LIVING & LOVING LOW FAT

By Tree Stevens

Foreword by Steven E. Swartz, M.D., F.A.C.S.

Living & Loving Low Fat

By Tree Stevens

Foreword by Steven E. Swartz, M.D., F.A.C.S.

Northwest Publishing, Inc.
Salt Lake City, Utah

Living & Loving Low-Fat

For information address: Northwest Publishing, Inc.
6906 South 300 West, Salt Lake City, Utah 84047
CR/JB 5-26-95

PRINTING HISTORY
First Printing 1995

ISBN: 1-56901-634-8

NPI books are published by Northwest Publishing, Incorporated,
6906 South 300 West, Salt Lake City, Utah 84047.
The name "NPI" and the "NPI" logo are trademarks belonging to
Northwest Publishing, Incorporated.

PRINTED IN THE UNITED STATES OF AMERICA.
10 9 8 7 6 5 4 3 2 1

This book is dedicated
to my David.

ACKNOWLEDGEMENTS

To those wonderful people who were there with help, inspiration and support, my deepest appreciation: Kathy Giordano, Debbie Gruberg, Jim Guynn, Ana Martinez, Jim Mann, Kim Brette Rubin, Meredith Bari Drescher, Edythe Eisenberg, Steve Stefanik, Dana McDonald, Nelda Caballero and Lou Cimaglia. To W. Norton McKinless, my special thanks for his creative input and his faith in the success of this project.

Credits

Illustrations and book design by Robert O. Shelley, Shelley Design, Baltimore, Maryland.

Photography by Don Carstens, Baltimore, Maryland.

TABLE OF CONTENTS

Table Of Contents

FOREWORD BY STEVEN E. SWARTZ, M.D., F.A.C.S.

Obesity is a growing problem in our society (forgive the pun). According to the National Center for Health Statistics, one-third of the U.S. population over age 20 is more than 20% overweight. This number has increased by 8% over the last 11 years in spite of the diet and exercise fads that have swept through this country since the 1970s. The seriousness of this problem is reflected in our current Health Care Crisis; the continuing upward spiral of the cost of health care is partially fueled by our increasing girth. Obesity is known or suspected to contribute to high blood pressure, diabetes, heart disease, breast, skin and colon cancer. Weight loss has been unquestionably shown to alleviate many of these, and frequently eliminate the need for costly drug treatments. So why do we stay fat?

The American Dream is NOT conducive to healthy living. Demanding careers and busy lifestyles leave less time for exercise and contribute to poor eating habits. Our leisure activities have become more passive and less active. Ironically, the decline of cigarette smoking nationwide, while healthy in itself, may explain some of our weight gain. We are also fortunate (or unfortunate) to have cheap, plentiful food supplies (high in fat and caloric content), as compared to the rest of the world. Our bounty may be our downfall.

Living & Loving Low Fat may be our savior.

Living & Loving Low Fat will help you understand eating, and dieting, and the reasons for failure. It focuses on staying away from the "temporary fix" and making the jump to a lifestyle adjustment that will result in a permanent weight reduction with easy maintenance. Isn't that what all the dieters have searched for?

This book describes a very simple-to-begin diet...limiting only fat intake. Since there are no other limitations there is no loss of nutrients or essential substances. The fat allowed is more than what is required daily, so there are no side effects. And the liberal portion sizes don't leave you hungry! The program actually encourages snacking to keep you satisfied and to promote fat utilization. The only intellectual effort needed is that required to read the food labels for fat content. The bonus is that the less fat present, the more you can eat!

I have not seen a simpler, easier, more pragmatic or healthier approach to weight loss. The only drawback is that no suffering is required, and this may deter those who feel they need to be punished for their obesity. The rest of us can enjoy the Good Taste, Good Life, and Good Health so splendidly described in *Living & Loving Low Fat*.

Assistant Professor of Surgery Uniformed Services
University of the Health Sciences

CHAPTER 1

YOU'D RATHER DIE THAN DIET?

FOOD!

Glorious. Delicious. Luscious. Delectable. Scrumptious. Succulent. Mouth-watering.

Read these words and you start salivating! There are so many ways to describe the pleasures of the palate. Eating is so much more than a necessary function of staying alive. Happy occasions, joyous times, celebrations of every kind, are closely linked with food. During times of bereavement and loss, there is the preparation of food to occupy us, and the sharing of love, through food, to console us. Food: sometimes elegant, sometimes traditional, sometimes basic, always important.

Our days revolve around mealtimes. For many families it is the only time there is conversation shared among family members. It's a gathering time for friends, and a meeting time for acquaintances, a tumultuous celebration dinner or an intimate candlelight dinner for lovers. Business is conducted at mealtime and our best deals are concluded at mealtime. Food is a major factor in many of our lives. We spend hours planning menus, searching out new recipes, shopping, preparing and serving. The holidays are specifically designated as "turkey-day" or require certain gastronomic specialties such as ham or fruitcake. The new neighbors are greeted with a platter of blueberry muffins, "Birthday" means ice cream and cake, and no Southerner can begin the New Year without blackeye peas. The statement, "we're going to eat…Chinese, or Japanese, or Greek, or Italian" food immediately conjures up tasty images you can feel melting in your mouth.

Ahhhh, food!

Consider the impact of what we eat on our lives. It's hard to separate the occasion from the food. At the same time, it's hard to separate the way we feel and the way we see ourselves from what we eat. For so many of us food is a motivator that started in childhood with the promise of a lollipop or, later, the payoff we allowed ourselves at the successful conclusion of a crash diet: a double-fudge sundae! There's the cycle of reward, calling for celebration and eating, followed by guilt, which calls for punishment and, therefore, denial and starvation, followed by boredom and, subsequently, the celebration or binge. There's the successful diet which results in the anticipated weight loss, the return to prior eating habits, followed by a weight gain greater than the loss, total frustration, subsequent binge…and then we do the same thing all over again. Sound familiar?

The yo-yo syndrome!

Identified for years as the villain in the nasty cycle of weight loss and eventual regain, with a slow-down of metabolism as a result, the veracity of this analysis is now in question. As explained in *Prevention Magazine*, November, 1987, in an article which quotes Dr. Theodore Van Itallie, the yo-yo syndrome has basis in scientific fact. As weight is lost fewer calories are burned because you're smaller; therefore, as you lose weight, your metabolic rate slows down. Eating too little can sabotage weight loss. The body feeds off protein when denied food and depleting muscle tissue can reduce the body's calorie-burning ability since muscle is the most metabolically active tissue. Also, a severely restricted diet trains the body to be more energy efficient, thereby conserving calories by slowing its resting metabolic rate and will usually stay depressed after normal eating patterns resume, according to George L. Blackburn, M.D., Ph.D., renowned obesity specialist who is associate professor of surgery at Harvard Medical School. Weight expert Wayne Callaway, M.D., associate clinical professor of medicine at George Washington University in Washington, D.C. has been quoted in *Prevention* as stating that women who have never dieted will do pretty well on a weight-loss program. It's the ones who dieted 40 times who have the most difficulty. Crash diets systematically set up a never-ending, never-winning cycle.

The *University of California at Berkeley Wellness Letter*, January, 1995, quotes a National Institutes of Health task force that found the "evidence for the claimed adverse health effects is not convincing or consistent." This contradicts previous evidence, as quoted in *The University of Texas Lifetime Health Letter*, November, 1993, that repeated loss and regaining of weight causes an increased risk of heart disease and death. So, even the experts disagree, except on one major issue. Slow, sustained weight loss, maintained over a period of time through changes in the fundamental approach to diet is healthy, even if the weight loss is less dramatic. The one point which is decidedly not in question is that weighing less is good for your health!

There are any number of magazines, newsletters, and digests out on the market dedicated to helping you improve your health, advising you how to look better while you're succeeding at feeling better, and offering you a slender body with the exercise of the month and a new diet with which you'll lose lots of pounds in a very short, painless period of time.

Where I grew up the expression that might fit here is: "From your lips to God's ears!"

Sure we all want to be healthy and fit, slim and trim. The ads show us beautiful people who have accomplished this magic balance of good looks and obvious perfection. But do you somehow get the feeling that perhaps these gorgeous people were born that way? I know I wasn't. If, in fact, you were...you have perfectly balanced cholesterol, your svelte figure shows not a hint of cellulite, your weight never varies more than a pound or two, there's not a blemish on your smooth, supple skin. You have a natural tan without the need of exposure to the rays of the sun, and your perfect build is a result of inherited muscle mass and sinew, rather than hours spent in a sweaty t-shirt in a crowded health club.

Unfortunately, most of us do not live the charmed existence we see the models enjoying on TV. Instead, we fight a continuing battle to look and feel good. How many fads have you found yourself following so that you could lose a pound here or a clothing size there? Do you remember the water diet? The grapefruit diet? The liquid meal diet? The high-protein low-carb diet? The low-protein high-carb diet? The fasting diet? The every-other-day diet?

Ah, yes, we've all been there. And most of us have gained back the weight faster than we'd lost it.

There are a number of people out there who have a wardrobe of clothes in different sizes reflecting the ups and downs of their waistline and derriere, a direct result of multiple diets' success or lack thereof. You can get it off. But, will it STAY off? And if your menu reflects the austere guidelines of "healthy" eating, can you withstand the temptations of the food you used to eat?

There was a time when, could I have had three wishes, I would have repeated the same wish three times...to eat all the food I enjoy, as much of it as I want, and maintain a slender, active, healthy body.

I am happy to say I have finally arrived!

The trip to this point has been filled with as many stumbles and falls as encountered by anyone who was brought up to love and worship FOOD! As a charter member of the Clean Plate Club, the four-food-group school of nutrition, and a victim of "the children who are starving in Europe" (the continent changes with each generation depending on the hardships suffered somewhere in the world), I was prepared at a young age for a life of frustration and starvation (in moderation, of course). Puberty was "plump" for me and I started my first diet at the age of twelve. There is no question but that a love-hate relationship had been developed between food and me. Sharing experiences with many people, I have found I'm not alone.

Am I still in love with food? You bet!

The gastronomical romance has certainly not died. That would be a major psychological adjustment for me, changing years of training. And I don't know that I would want to change this relationship between oral satisfaction and my sense of well-being. It would be a disaster to forbid the emotional attachment we all have to using food when happy or sad, to feel happier or not quite so sad.

What I have done is change the KIND of food I turn to for the "feel goods." And the greatest benefit from this change has been happening to me inside as well as outside. Looking good, walking with a bounce in my step, feeling lean, these things are all important and are a big part of my overall well-being and happiness. After having had the awful pronouncement made to me, following surgery on my thyroid, that there was, in fact, a malignant tumor found, enjoying robust good health, and surpassing the stamina of many people younger than I am, is a blast!

And this happy state of being is easily achievable for you, too.

Chapter II

Why Me?

This book is about FIGHTING FAT. How to get rid of fat, how to keep fat off and how to live without fat.

Yes, you've heard all those great promises before. You've probably read all those books on dieting, on exercise, on losing weight and on being slim, trim and generally irresistible, that crowd the non-fiction section of the book stores. Some may have made it to your own bookshelves. That's why I've decided to share with you this gratifying lifestyle that will lead to a thinner, healthier, happier you. While you achieve your lifelong goals of losing fat with no fear of regaining it, you will feel better and improve your chances for a longer life. At the same time, you will never feel deprived. You will eat more than you ever have before and wonder where the fat went!

At the same time you will learn how easy…really easy…it is to do! Easy on your psyche because there is no deprivation; easy on your wallet, because you will spend less on food and exercise than you ever considered possible; and easy on your schedule because you'll be introduced to recipes for foods that are delicious and take very little time to prepare. Doesn't that sound wonderful?

There has been a stampede to present methods that accomplish these goals and they are popping up on the stores' shelves all over the country, talking about fat and the need to reduce the amount you eat. The question is, "Can you fit these tenets into YOUR life?"

The answer is, "You bet you can!"

The best news is, the lifestyle I describe throughout this book is easy livin'. There are changes you'll make…but changes are necessary whenever you enter into a new lifestyle. Are these changes traumatic? I didn't think so. Many who have tried this new approach to eating tell me they've had no problems adjusting.

Obviously, you are interested in your shape and the state of your health because you have this book in your hands. And you probably already know that the diet emphasis today is on fat consumption rather than calorie consumption. It takes very little energy to transform dietary fat to body fat. Calories from carbohydrates take five times as much energy to store. It has been determined that fat is the culprit in heart disease; cancer of the breast, uterus, prostate and colon; high blood pressure; diabetes; atherosclerosis; stroke and obesity. While there are contributing factors in each of these diseases, fat is a significant player. The American Heart Association, the American Diabetes Association and the American Cancer Society are all in agreement on the need for Americans to reduce the amount of fat in their diet to help fight these dread diseases. In fact, there are indications that a low-fat diet promotes clearer thinking and helps avoid the ravages of old-age memory loss.

In those countries where the average diet is lower in fat than our own, the incidence of these diseases is lower as well. *Lancet*, May 18, 1991 reported a study of 200 pre-menopausal Singapore women whose incidence of breast cancer was directly affected by changes in their diet. Increasing consumption of animal proteins and red meat, and therefore dietary fat, was associated with elevated risk of the disease.

Dr. Peter Greenwald of the National Cancer Institute has stated that if American women ate a diet that was as low in fat as the Japanese, instead of the 45,000 breast cancer deaths a year, there would be 8,000 to 10,000 deaths, as there are in Japan. The Japanese diet is acknowledged as lower in fat than our own, with emphasis on grains and vegetables, with meats used primarily as a condiment, and the Orientals do not suffer the same high rates of the aforementioned diseases we do. As the Japanese diet becomes more Americanized, the incidence of these diseases has been increasing.

As outlined in an article which appeared in *Prevention*, February, 1992, a drastic cut in fat consumption resulted in improved blood cholesterol readings (as you know, an important measure of the body's susceptibility to heart disease and high blood pressure). Heart patients who had altered their diet to one extremely low in fat enjoyed a 91% reduction in chest pains and had more energy, could think more clearly, and generally felt better.

If better health does not present enough reason to prompt you to think of changing your lifestyle, this finding might! A study mentioned in *Metabolism*, September, 1990, showed that a high-fat diet may negatively influence sexuality. Four hours following having drunk a high-fat shake, a group of men reacted with a 30% reduction in testosterone. The control group consumed a low-fat drink of carbohydrates and protein and experienced no change in the level of the hormone. Testosterone affects sex drive in both men and women. The assumption is that indulgence in fatty foods, and the subsequent hormonal reduction, would affect women in the same way. That's motivation!

I've seen references to a low-fat diet as the diet for disease prevention! Literature abounds advocating the need to reduce fat consumption amid estimates of the ill effects of overindulgence in fat-containing foods. These articles use terms such as cholesterol, polyunsaturates, monounsaturates, saturated fats, percentages of fats to calories with a plethora of graphs and ratios to help readers achieve the recommended balance of fats, fiber and calories. The FDA has even changed the age-old model of the original four basic food groups from a circle to a pyramid, with no- and low-fat foods at the base and fat foods at the pinnacle, to emphasize the high risk of fat in the health equation. Most people desiring healthier eating habits in keeping with those findings have a problem deciphering what they can do to make these necessary adjustments to their lives and diets.

There's got to be a simple, sensible, enjoyable approach to eating well and eating right! It sometimes takes a person untrained in the scientific field of diet and nutrition to present an understandable, unpretentious, hands-on "how-to," in plain language, to bridge the gap between science and application. This book is your gap-filler.

My credentials are as simple as is my approach. Finding a way to become and stay slender, skinny enough to look "good" in today's society, is a lifetime preoccupation. I have been aware of every new approach to that goal, investigated all types of fads, hypes, to-do's and not-to-do's and, I admit it...I have become obsessed. Finding answers leading to better health as well as weight control was a fortunate accident.

I was lucky. It was a roller coaster...the same one experienced by many of you who are reading this book. You are probably nodding your head because you've tried a number of different methods of dropping a pound, twenty or fifty. Like you, I was going to find a remarkable method to enjoy staying slim, forever! There was even hope of a magic elixir that would allow me to eat anything I wanted, keep what my body needed, and discard any excess. Although this dream has not yet been realized (they're working on it right now!) I think I've come close—without the elixir.

The roller coaster ride came to a screeching halt, in 1986, when a hefty young man who worked out in the same athletic club as I, entered the club noticeably trimmer. Always anxious to hear the details of any successful weight loss program, I conducted an in-depth cross examination. Jack was more than happy to share his secrets, as are most of us in the "fight the fat" forum. He told me he fought the fat by eliminating high-fat foods from his diet, and reducing his fat intake to a prescribed number of grams. He was limited to no more than 20 grams of fat per day.

I watched Jack maintain his new weight. He said he felt better than he'd ever felt before, and watching him work out, this energy was apparent. Besides, he looked great!

No sooner had he confided in me than I, a tried-and-true diet-doer, had to do it, too! I learned from him the same kind of information available in popular publications today. He was just a few years ahead of the trend. Here was a better way! And an intensive food analysis was begun.

This was especially interesting to me because I was aware of the studies on breast cancer that had been circulated for quite some time promoting a low fat diet. As a victim of fibrocystic disease of the breast, and having had many biopsies, I flirted with the idea of reducing fat in my diet. One tumor, removed in 1979, was diagnosed as "pre-cancerous." Now here was a way to accomplish two important goals: fight fat on the outside of my body, while I fight cancer on the inside of my body.

Years of programming had to be radically modified! I stopped counting calories. I altered my eating habits with the help of a comprehensive food counter book. I never looked at the calorie column, and was eating more than ever before! There was total abstinence here, and substitution there, yet I was not merely maintaining my weight, I was actually losing weight, and I was never hungry! IT WORKED!

Anyone who has spent years fighting the ups and downs of the scales, or who has watched family and friends suffer this plight, has an obligation to share the solution to the problem. Those who have valiantly waged the war against weight gain are always ready to try another method of dieting, looking for the one that will result in permanent weight loss. Since 1987, the people with whom I've shared this way of controlling weight have had the same positive results I've had. Weight loss followed by easily managed weight maintenance. The amounts and kinds of foods you eat do not change, whether you are losing or maintaining weight, thereby eliminating the frustrating weight gain which immediately follows most diets.

While the articles and reports in the media all endorse this healthier lifestyle, the information and methodology is presented in such a confusing, contradictory and complicated manner that it would discourage most people from making the attempt at deciphering the information to begin with. You are informed by the FDA guidelines (those "Nutrition Facts" they've introduced on the labels of your favorite products) that your fat intake should be 30% of your caloric intake. Others claim the only way to see an appreciative difference in weight or health is 20% to 25%. That's great! What should the caloric intake be? What if you want to lose weight and know your caloric intake is too high? What do you do with the fat percentage?

Among the instructions for determining fat percentages is to check the labels for total grams of fat per serving, then multiply that number by nine, divide by the total calories per serving, and multiply by one hundred. Dr. Steven Swartz, a surgeon, an expert in geriatric nutrition and formerly a surgeon in the United States Navy, says the caloric "average" on the FDA labels from which the recommended percentage is derived (2000 calories per day) is enough to sustain a marine during intensive training. How many of us expend that kind of energy in a normal day? One article I read suggested that a woman who weighs 130 pounds can eat 1600 calories per day to maintain that weight. Therefore, if you want to weigh 130 pounds, reduce your fat intake to 30% of that caloric intake, divide by nine (the amount of calories in one fat gram) and you have your fat gram allotment to effect the necessary weight loss to reach the goal of 130 pounds: 54 grams of fat per day!

The variables are overwhelming. Perhaps you don't burn calories as efficiently as that 130 pound woman being used as your standard. You could conceivably gain weight consuming 54 grams of fat a day. I would!

If this is not sufficiently confusing, there are all those products appearing on the supermarket shelves claiming how "low" or "no" fat they are, while there are those experts in the news media and magazines warning you not to be fooled...those products will make you gain weight, anyhow! Evidently, the assumption is that rather than a slice of pie à la mode, you are going to eat an entire Entenmann's Fat-Free Cherry Beehive Pie because it's fat-free, topped with at least a quart of Sealtest Fat-Free Ice Cream. Common sense still dictates smart eating, even while you indulge yourself. The idea is to enjoy the foods you love to eat without consuming the 18 grams of fat in a slice of Mrs. Smith's Cherry Pie and 13 fat grams in 1/2 cup (2 scoops) of Baskin Robbins vanilla ice cream. Your Entenmann's slice of pie and Sealtest Ice Cream, if you choose their fat-free products, are safe and slim!

The information I've acquired, and the answers I've accumulated, can make the transition to a low-fat diet easy. The lifestyle I'm about to outline can trim you down, and improve your health—naturally. A situation seldom achieved with those crash diets you've suffered before. Without the use of a calculator you will be able to adjust your eating habits for the long term. Since this is not a fad or crash diet you will not experience frustration and loss of confidence by gaining back more weight than you'd lost nor will it present a hardship for you as you've encountered so many times before when embarking on a new "diet." If you are initiating a change of eating habits to enhance your cholesterol, you need not fear the dreaded uninviting "blahs" that have been dished out for you in the past in the name of good health. Instead you'll find yourself replacing foods you've always enjoyed by foods you'll enjoy even more. You'll also see how to adjust the recipes of old favorites so that they fit your new lifestyle.

Prompted by the need for variety and truly enjoyable meals and menus, I started collecting and altering recipes to fit the lifestyle, and subsequently created a number of recipes as well. You'll find these later on in the book and you'll be surprised at how quickly you'll be inventing dishes yourself to suit your own individual tastes.

Enough time has been spent on old tried-and-failed methods. Let's get down to the nitty-gritty! The first step is to remove all the information stored for years in your head about dieting. Open your mind and accept an easy and satisfying way to lose weight and help your body to become healthier and stay healthier!

CHAPTER III

THINK FAT—GET THIN

The war on fat is on! Everywhere you look there are reports, articles, publications and books referring to fat, whether it is in regard to health or weight control. Everyone is talking about their cholesterol, the HDL, the LDL, triglycerides, plaques. Because the media has emphasized the damage that saturated fat can have on our health, we are faced with myriad concerns: Does a product contain polyunsaturated or saturated fats?

Do monounsaturates lower your LDL or raise your HDL? Which foods are "good" for you? Which are not? Which fats are "good" for you or are all fats "bad" for you? In a labeling effort to sell more product, the packaging experts throw the word FREE on packages: 97% Fat FREE, 85% Fat FREE, Cholesterol FREE. None of these packages informs the consumer exactly what the product is free from! One product on the supermarket shelf brags it is FREE in jumbo, neon letters across the top of the package. On close inspection one finds it is free of saturated fat, but extremely high in unsaturated fats. Not an attractive product for those looking for FAT-FREE. And what does all this mean, anyway?

The need for a diet low in fat may not be shared by everyone, but as pointed out in Chapter I, the American Cancer Society, the American Heart Association and the American Diabetes Association are among those recommending dietary fat control for a healthier you. Many of the people who must alter their lifestyle to embrace a low fat regimen are forced to make this decision for medical reasons rather than by the desire for weight loss.

Let's look for a moment at what your system does with fat. What are the value differences between fat and carbohydrates? Dr. Gabe Mirkin presents a compelling argument in favor of carbohydrates over fats, when considering indulgence, in his book, *Getting Thin, All About Fat*, Little Brown, in which he compares the caloric value of carbohydrates, at 4.5 calories per gram, to that of fats, at 9 calories per gram. Simple logic dictates you can eat about twice the quantity of carbohydrates than fats for the same calorie count. But it doesn't stop there. He refers to the greater volume of food one can eat when consuming complex carbohydrates, such as fruits, vegetables, grains and legumes as compared to fatty foods, not only because of the double calorie count in fat grams, but because of the density of foods high in fat. A small bag of M&M's Peanuts, 1.74 ounces, contains 250 calories. A pound of apples contains 242 calories. Add to these factors that it takes more calories to burn carbs as energy. Since fat is utilized more efficiently it is easier to store in all those cute places we'd rather not talk about. It takes more grams of carbohydrates to store the same amount of fat. In other words, when you eat fat...it shows.

While we're talking about efficiency, this is a good time to note another important factor regarding calorie burning.

All of you who skip breakfast, please stand up!

During the time you're so proud of yourself for not introducing more calories to your system, your poor old regulator thinks you're starving, and shuts down. For the rest of the day, while you think you're conserving on your calorie intake, your body is busy storing, not burning. Your machine will make you work harder to burn those calories than if you had kept your engine stoked from early morning.

A study reported in the *American Journal of Clinical Nutrition*, March 1992, illustrated that obese women who ate breakfast lost more weight than obese women who consumed the same amount of calories but who skipped breakfast.

Eating six to eight small meals, or even nibbling all day, will boost the metabolism, causing it to burn much more efficiently, thereby helping you to lose weight more rapidly. Dr. Gabe Mirkin, in the *Mirkin Report*, March 1992, states that "nibblers have less body fat and lower cholesterol." There is data that shows a higher metabolic rate two to three hours after food is ingested. Eating small meals throughout the day will help to rekindle that burn as you progress through the day. And, once this pattern is developed, you'll have a hard time going back to one or two "big" meals a day. An interesting benefit of this kind of nibble-nourish is the avoidance of that famished feeling after having gone for six hours with nothing in your tummy. Since it takes twenty minutes to register satiety, you're so hungry when you finally do eat you consume a much greater quantity, much more quickly, and by the time your brain gets the message that you've had enough to eat, you've had too much! In fact, a useful strategy to avoid eating the wrong foods at a party, or too much of the goodies that aren't good for you, is to enjoy a satisfying nibble before you go. That way you "take the edge off" your hunger and you can be a more discerning guest.

CHAPTER IV

GO FOR THE BURN

When we talk about burn, there's another kind of burn that cannot be neglected in any writing about losing weight or, for that matter, maintaining health. Yup! You guessed it! We must talk about exercise!

Each of us, at one time or another, has made the sacrifice and put aside the time to accommodate a morning or afternoon run or gym visit. Those of us who have are all too familiar with the reasons not to. "There's no time for exercise." "It never worked for me." "Working out made me gain weight." "I hurt myself."

There are as many excuses as there are unused lifetime athletic club memberships! Unfortunately, however inventive the reasoning for not exercising may be, the reasons for it are overwhelmingly compelling.

To be succinct, exercise gives the engine a kick-start and helps keep the motor running. Physically and mentally! The benefits from exercise, the metabolic rate increase, the increased energy, and the good feeling, last for hours. The thirty minutes you donate to a brisk walk, or the bike, or an energetic dance routine, will continue to burn calories for you for four to six hours. And as you build new muscle, you'll burn even more calories because muscle burns more energy than fat. The mere exchange of muscle for fat will help you to metabolize what you eat more efficiently, help you slim down faster and maintain the slim "you" better.

According to the *Journal of Clinical Nutrition*, exercise offers the only way to eat more and lose weight. The wonderful addendum to that is that exercise is a natural appetite suppressant. It is, simultaneously, a mood elevator as a result of increasing the level of endorphins, the natural painkiller in the brain that generates feelings of well-being.

If your motivation is purely to enhance your health, there can be no better medicine for your body. Consider the changes in recent years in caring for a patient following a heart attack. Now, that patient is walking the next day! Not even back problems will allow us bed-rest anymore. The advice to sufferers with knee damage is to build the muscle surrounding the knee and thereby provide better support for the knee. How can one consider himself fit without a bit of the "burn?"

The workout we're talking about does not call for an expensive spa membership (although that's nifty) nor a myriad of jazzy machines and weights, or a pair of $250.00

shoes! A religious, 30 minute, large-muscle workout, performed every other day, will get the fat-burners revved up, and simultaneously do wonders for your health. The experts from Dr. Mirkin and Dr. Blackburn to Joseph Piscatella (*Controlling Your Fat Tooth*, Workman Publishing), and the publications from *Prevention* to *American Health Magazine*, all agree on the need for large-muscle (those in your legs and back) exercise to achieve cardiovascular fitness, burn calories, fight osteoporosis and postpone aging. These simple and enjoyable activities include BRISK walking (not necessarily jogging, which is harder on the body), bicycling (indoors or out), cross-country skiing (indoors or on the slopes), aerobic dancing (or any kind of energetic dancing such as square dancing), stair-walking (or a stepper), rowing or trampoline jumping. There is, in New York, a studio that teaches Karate moves with the aerobics to give the students a three-fold benefit: the increased heart-rate of any aerobics class, the opportunity to vent frustrations in more aggressive movements, and the added confidence one derives from being able to properly defend oneself. Isn't that a great idea?

The purpose of these exercises is to increase your pulse to a desirable rate for the sustained period of 30 minutes. There are charts available to show the proper heart rate range for individuals in varying age groups. Many instructors believe, however, that if you are performing with an increased heart rate rapid enough to feel the change in the pulse at your throat with your fingertips, yet you have sufficient control of your breath to converse with someone, you're in the proper target zone for sustained aerobic benefit. If you cannot control your breathing well enough to talk with someone else, you've passed the point of aerobic exercise and entered an anaerobic state. Slow down until you once more gain control. The experts recommend letting your body dictate the intensity of your workout. You'll find yourself increasing intensity and extending the time you work out as you become accustomed to exercising. Start out slowly with 10 or 15 minutes of a routine modified to a beginner and gradually increase as you improve.

Take time to warm up and cool down, in addition to the 30 minutes of your more intense workout. Listen to your body and stop if you hurt. No pain, no gain is a way to court injury. By pushing too hard, and trying to reach the next level too fast, you may find yourself, instead, healing from an injury.

My best friend, David, used to live five minutes from the "Club." At 5:30 in the morning he was at their door ready to wake up with the morning news while he pumped away on the Lifecycle. Every other day he'd include a round of weights and resistance equipment. After the workout he'd shmoose with the guys over a cup of coffee. And, then one day, he moved to another city where there were no nearby clubs and those he found opened at 7:00 a.m. No time to exercise in the morning and no desire to work out in the afternoon. For four years he let it go, when one day he recognized how stiff he'd been feeling and how touching his toes had become a major feat (if he could manage it, at all). He started a simple 10 minute regimen of stretching exercises, gradually increasing intensity and adding more complicated positions, some tummy crunches, and eventually some weights. The workout is at home, now, as early as he likes...and he's even added a stop at a local diner where he meets the guys for some coffee and conversation before the workday starts. Oh, by the way, he can touch his toes!

The workout that works must be one that fits you! It must fit both your purse and your schedule. If the country club or fancy fitness club, for which you must get dolled up to get sweaty, does not give you a rush, try this easy approach to revving up the motor. Start off with the purchase of an aerobic "step." There are many brands available in sports shops and there are a few offered on TV. The prices start as low as $30.00. Buy a pair of ankle weights and wrist weights and two dumbbells to which you can add weight. This regimen is one that includes the necessary aerobics with weight-bearing exercises.

You work up to 30 minutes a day, 3 days a week, on the step, utilizing a basic, alternating step, up and down. No need to get fancy. The aerobic benefits from 30 minutes of stepping is equivalent to about 50 flights up and down a 14-step staircase. You can start with 5 minutes and increase as you become accustomed to the workout. On alternate days, 2 or 3 days a week, use your step for 20 minutes and add 15 to 20 minutes of dumbbell work to strengthen your arms, shoulders and back. You'll eventually be spending 30 minutes 3 days a week and 40-50 minutes 2 or 3 days a week to accomplish all you need to aerobisize and tighten up. Add 5-10 minutes of tummy work on your short days and you'll be gorgeous and healthy in no time.

This workout equipment takes very little space, about 2 feet by 3 feet, and since you can pop out of bed and watch the early morning news while you do it, there is no great expenditure of time. There are no tights or thongs to buy. A t-shirt, shorts or sweat-pants, and workout shoes are all you need. Oh, yes, don't forget a pair of socks. You'll find the socks with the cushiony sole feel really good.

If you prefer an evening workout, do your thing while dinner is microwaving. You know, one of those one-dish meals you prepared over the weekend that was "ready to go" for a delicious, quickie reheat tonight (recipes follow!).

Be sure to check with your doctor before beginning any new workout regimen.

Does exercise work? You bet it does! Can you spare one and a half to three hours per week, broken up into thirty minute segments? You bet you can!

Over the long haul, there is no combination to better aid in weight loss or the maintenance of weight loss, and to add healthful active years to your life, than eating properly and exercising energetically and consistently. There are loads of books, videos, and TV programs, as well, on the subject. Common sense, however, and the consensus of medical opinion, opt for a forty-eight hour rest for muscles between workouts, and suggest using a variety of routines that you will enjoy.

Although a thirty-minute period, three times a week, will do the job aerobically, there are those people who find a daily workout is easier to handle. It works better for them because it affords them a time of privacy, a time during which they are doing something good for themselves, from which they will benefit the rest of the day. Spending the same time of the day, every day, on exercise, helps it to become automatic...simply a part of the daily schedule. If you are one of those organized people, change the muscle group you concentrate on, so that on alternate days you're using a different set of muscles, giving each group a forty-eight hour rest. If you use weights, skip a day before repeating an upper body workout. Do some floor work on your legs and tush, as an alternative, to avoid injury. And choose forms of exercise you enjoy! That way you'll continue doing them. Don't forget there's that psychological lift in addition to the metabolic lift. You'll feel so much better on your workout days, you'll WANT to work out five or six times a week!

CHAPTER V

A SIMPLE RULE

You don't want fat ON your body. You don't want fat IN your body. So stop putting so much fat in your mouth! And start burning the fat you've already stored so it is gone for good.

The whole idea is not to diet it off, but rather, to eat it off! And continue to eat the same way to keep it off. That way you're not looking at a quickie fix that will reverse itself as soon as you go back to "normal eating" because this way of eating is, from now on, "normal eating" for you! And you need NEVER BE HUNGRY!

Without question, one of the most self-destructive feelings in the world is walking away from a feast, feeling famished, and while everyone else gorges on goodies, you're "good" and hungry! Then you've become so frustrated and feel so deprived that when you do allow yourself to eat until you're full, you just keep on eating until you've more than made up for the empties and you're disgusted with yourself. This dilemma is a thing of the past. From now on you will have so many foods to choose from which are low in fat, you can fill up on these, ignore those that are taboo, and leave the table satisfied with no guilt.

The average American consumes approximately 65 to 85 grams of fat a day! Some people burn off more than others do, and, as you well know, some people just "look at food and gain weight." By restricting your intake of fat you'll become a burner, too.

How many grams of fat a day should a person take in to stay healthy, lose extra pounds, and then healthfully maintain an appropriate weight?

The young man, Jack, to whom I referred earlier who originally introduced me to this way of life, confined himself to 20 fat grams per day. At the Pritikin Longevity Center in Santa Monica, California, a combination spa/cardiac-rehabilitation center, the diet is limited to a 10% fat-to-calorie ratio. In the *Mirkin Report*, November, 1990, Dr. Gabe Mirkin states, "How much fat should you eat? Fewer than 20 grams of fat daily while maintaining a sensible calorie intake to reduce weight, cholesterol, blood pressure and risk of heart disease and cancer." That sounds like a low number compared to the average American consumption, doesn't it? It is. But it's not hard to do. There are some simple methods to follow which we'll talk about. And then...you're on your way.

Aha! At this moment your tongue rolls into your cheek, the eyebrows rise, and thoughts of, "What do I have to do?" or more accurately, "Do without?" fill your head. For years, there's been the vicious cycle established of reward and punishment. You've spent years consuming those foods you crave, and then enduring the punishment of the inevitable diet. This pain is followed by the reward of knowing you've reached your goal or the frustration of not having accomplished what you'd set out to do. Either way you have reason to splurge! On the one hand, to celebrate, on the other, as solace. This gratification is inexorably followed by guilt, which can be assuaged only by punishment. The punishment is the stricter, more painful denial of the foods you crave. This binge/guilt/punish cycle must come to an end for a person to be consistently happy when they sit at the table, or want a nibble. That is what this book is all about. So, relax. Enjoy.

There is only one major rule. You want to stay at or below 20 grams of fat a day.

There are three ways to accomplish this:

READ LABELS

Manufacturers of food products now include a breakdown of values on the label such as calories, sodium, fiber and fat grams. This information is a requirement of any packaged product you purchase. And using this breakdown properly will help make the transition to this lifestyle much easier.

When reading the label, your only concern is the fat gram count. The listing usually applies to only one serving. Be sure to calculate the correct amount of fat grams for the amount of servings you are consuming. For example, one serving of pretzels may be one ounce, but how many ounces are you eating? A can of Campbell's Condensed New

England Clam Chowder has only 3 grams per serving. But did you know that there are 2 3/4 servings in each can? Multiply the number of ounces or servings by the fat gram count per serving. The number per serving or per ounce multiplied by the amount consumed is part of your fat gram quota for the day, which will not exceed 20 grams.

One way to approach the fat grams you're consuming in a packaged product is to multiply the total ounces by the fat grams per ounce or the total servings of the package by the fat gram count per serving. Then work backward when deciding whether you want to consume the whole can of Progresso Healthy Classics Minestrone Soup and its 4 grams of fat or, on the other hand, portion out half of the box of SnackWell's Cheese Crackers which is half of the 11 grams in the whole box!

Remember not to fall victim to the "95% Fat Free" claims which are so common. Read carefully, so you are truly aware of the fat content of a product, in grams. Do not be concerned about the percentages because, as we had discussed earlier, we do not believe that 60 grams of fat a day is acceptable. In addition, there is just too much math involved!

If the label does not spell out for you the total fat grams per serving, read the ingredients on the product label. If there are any oils listed, you then have to decide whether you want to take the chance of assuming the fat content of the oil according to the placement of the listing. Keep in mind that 1 tablespoon of oil has 14 grams of fat, regardless of the type oil it is: olive, safflower, vegetable or canola. Ingredients in any product are listed in order, according to volume. The first listing represents the largest quantity and the last represents the smallest. I prefer to play it safe and avoid guesswork. Keep looking for a brand that either spells out the fat gram content for you, is listed in the fat gram counter book by brand name, or make it from scratch! In time, you'll become familiar with the foods and brands you purchase most often, and this procedure will become much easier.

USE A PAPERBACK FOOD COUNTER BOOK

Until you become accustomed to your new lifestyle and the contents of the foods you eat most often, this book will be invaluable. The good ones out there include name brands that may not have detailed labeling; fresh foods (such as fruits, vegetables, meats, poultry, seafood, cheeses, etc.); and fast food values to help you quickly determine what to order when you're at McDonald's or Wendy's. After a while, you won't have to look it up. The fat grams of your favorite foods will become as much a part of you as your name and date of birth.

It would be a good idea to inventory your shelves and refrigerator, using your counter book, to help you separate the foods that are part of your new lifestyle from those you will give away to friends and neighbors who are not yet eating smart. You'll be amazed at how rapidly you'll acquire an appreciation for those foods that are smart foods. By all means, take your counter book with you on your initial shopping trips.

Two good counter books are: *The Complete Book of Food Counts* by Corinne T. Netzer, published by Dell and *The Complete & Up-To-Date Fat Book* by Karen J. Bellerson, published by Avery Publishing Group. These books can be found in any of the popular book stores in your area. They are both soft-covered books.

INCREASE FRUITS, VEGETABLES, GRAINS AND LEGUMES

The advantage of eating fruits and veggies is how good for you they are and how low in fat they are! In years gone by you probably shunned potatoes, beans and corn to keep the calories in line, thereby avoiding a perfect source of protein and fiber. Never mind the fact that these veggies taste so good and are so satisfying. So many people have asked me how you dress these foods up to fit the tastes we've acquired over the years. How do you eat a baked potato, dry? As you recall, I promised that you would enjoy what you eat. The doodads that you will use to glamorize your vegetables are available to you later on in the book, so you needn't worry about eating that potato without the good stuff. What you should do, in the beginning, is check out the fat gram count of those vegetables that are already an important part of your diet. That way you'll start with a good idea of the basics. These foods, with few exceptions, are very low in fat, most of them providing mere traces at the most, and can be prepared in delicious, filling, satisfying recipes. You'll find a bunch of them included in the recipe section of this book. You'll be pleasantly surprised!

There you have three simple instructions to facilitate your entrance into a new world of gastronomic pleasures. There are so many wonderful-tasting delicacies that will be introduced to you because of your new way of eating. Of course, you may have trepidation about starting this lifestyle. After all, you've built a lifetime of habit into your food preferences. You like what you eat. That's why you eat it! What you eat is important to you! And, in this, you are not alone. We are all protective of satisfying habits that obviously make us feel comfortable. That's one of the reasons so many of us use food to satisfy our need for the "warm fuzzies." The whole idea here is to satisfy these needs and do so within the 20 grams of fat, or less, a day. Yes! You can do it!

Hold everything! What about portion-sizes? What about calories? How can an individual successfully "diet" without cutting out and cutting down? How can any person lose weight without counting calories?

My previous allegations that you can ENJOY this "lifestyle" while losing weight and improving your health may have sounded like just so much hokum. If you're a practiced dieter, you've heard this kind of claim before and, as we talked about earlier, found the weight returning faster than its departure. One of those diets that enjoyed great popularity, perhaps because it required no calorie-counting or quantity-control, was "Dr. Stillman's Quick Weight-Loss Diet." A high-protein diet that was based on all-you-can-eat meats, it was a quick weight-loss success. Since a human being, however, needs carbohydrates to survive healthfully and the fat content of this diet was extremely high, a long-term regimen was not recommended. The return to "normal" eating produced the steady return to previous "normal" weight levels. A grand success, if your weight-loss was for a particular occasion and you didn't have the desire to maintain the loss, afterward.

Is not the same problem encountered here? For a number of reasons, the answer is, NO! Most compelling is the explanation of Dr. Martin Katahn, author of *The T-Factor Diet*, (W.W. Norton & Co., Inc.) who refers to the difference in the metabolizing of carbohydrates as compared to fats. "The cost of converting dietary fat to body fat is only 3 percent," he writes, "which means that only 3 out of every 100 calories of dietary fat will be burned as the body converts fat for storage. In comparison, the cost of going through the various steps that convert carbohydrate to fat is about 25 percent...the body finds a way to burn off just about every single bit of the carbohydrate you give it or enter it into temporary glycogen storage, and only the fat goes to fat. Under normal circumstances, in any given day, a maximum of only about 4 percent of the carbohydrate is converted to fat."

In addition, if you were to keep a count of the calories ingested in a typical day of your 20-gram lifestyle, you'd find a much reduced caloric total compared to that of the higher caloric content of the fat-dense, low-bulk foods in your previous diet. This, in fact, will become apparent to you when you look at the total fat grams in each of the recipes that follow in this book and compare the caloric values, using your food-counter book, to the same type foods which are not prepared in the low-fat manner. In other words, you can eat a heck of a lot more and keep (on your body) a heck of a lot less.

It is for the reasons defined above that you will find no calorie count along with the fat gram count following each recipe, or portion-size accountability required when you eat the low-fat way.

Are you responsible for using good judgment?

Always!

As pointed out to you earlier in the book, in Chapter II, if you choose to enjoy a slice of Entenmann's Fat-Free Beehive Cherry Pie with a scoop of Sealtest Vanilla Fat-Free Ice Cream and it tastes so good you devour the whole pie and a quart of the ice cream, you may be eating "no-fat," but you are hurting yourself and over-indulgence will defeat your purpose in this, or any healthy, lifestyle. But a slice of that pie with a hefty scoop of the ice cream will not hurt your fat, or food, intake for the day one bit, and will keep you on balance, helping you to avoid the food frenzy of the deprived.

When you are eating a bowl of pasta with a sauce that has only traces of fat, the size of the portion is immaterial because the bulk of the food ingested will satisfy your appetite before the caloric value can get out of hand. Two cups of egg-free pasta has less than 1-1/2 grams of fat and 384 calories. A one-half cup serving of the sauce, prepared fat-free, is only 60 calories, or less. Add the meats and fats to the sauce and you add the stuff that will add the pounds. Lean ground beef (21% fat), 4 ounces, uncooked, has 24 grams of fat, 303 calories. Each tablespoon of olive oil has 14 grams of fat, 120 calories. The mushrooms, onions, green peppers and garlic are virtually fat-free and 1 cup of each of the vegetables with 1 clove of garlic total less than 100 calories!

You CAN enjoy this lifestyle without analyzing your calorie consumption or portion-size by keeping your fat-gram count at 20 or less!

CHAPTER VI

THIS IS A DIET?

By taking a look at the three, or more, meals that you now enjoy in a day, you will see some of the differences you'll encounter at first. Have no fear. The people who specialize in behavioral science say that three to six weeks with a new regimen is all that's necessary for most human beings to accept change and begin to incorporate the new behavior as habit. Obviously, one of the reasons the old fad diets didn't work was that there was never an attempt at making those "unnatural" plans, habit. It's unnatural to live on liquid meals, or carry a scale with you to a restaurant, or leave the table hungry enough for dinner, even though you've had your three grapes and 4 lettuce leaves.

The meals we will discuss are ideas for you to consider incorporating into your daily diet. These are, however, merely ideas. How you decide to arrive at your 20, or fewer, grams of fat per day is all your baby. As you've already learned, it's important to eat at least three times a day, preferably more frequently, to keep your battery charged and your metabolism on high. You don't want your body to think you're starving and start storing.

You'll find, as well, that one advantage of this way of eating is in helping to regulate the bowels, as a result of the high fiber ingested. This alone, for some, is cause for making this lifestyle a habit. Fiber, a major part of vegetables, grains and legumes, has another advantage for the person trying to lose weight: you get very little value from fiber, since it is not digestible. As it passes through your intestines, it picks up and carries with it some fat which has not yet been digested, removing both from your body without adding anything to your system but bulk, which you expel.

There are strategies for accomplishing the goal we've set and for making this whole new experience easier for you. Preparation of the meals you'll be adding to your menus must be simple because your time is precious. The basic ethnicity of your diet must stay essentially the same because you are you, and you must stay basically the same. This is important in order that you stick with it and not feel as though this is a short term fix, rather than a lifestyle adjustment. However, you will probably add some neat, new dishes to your present diet. There are wonderful foods you've never tasted waiting for you to enjoy!

While choosing the foods to be included in your repertoire, you want to be sure to try different products and recipes. Boredom, as you know, will sabotage your desire to continue eating this way. The success of this lifestyle is satisfaction! In the food you eat, in how you look, and in the way you feel. So be a little adventurous as you become accustomed to the gram counts. Try some of the tricks for good eating you'll find later on in the book and, by all means, give some of the recipes a go!

Mel, who started this lifestyle not long ago, said he's always had a problem with flatulence and would skip the bean dishes. That would surely be a shame. Not only do they taste good, but the bean is a good source of protein, fiber and nutrients, hard to compare with any other food. The problem of flatulence is shared by many. If you've avoided beans in the past, there is a product on the market called "Beano" that provides the enzyme which, when ingested, will allow you to digest properly the part of the bean that causes the gas build-up. Then you can enjoy those recipes, too, to your heart's content. Give the "Beano" folks a call at 1-800-257-8650 and they'll be happy to tell you more about their product.

It appears that one of the major problems in choosing dishes to add to your menus is the overwhelming confusion at where to begin. This has deterred many who, although seemingly serious about changing their eating habits to control fat, give up for lack of information about the foods they may and may not eat. You'll find some ideas that may be new to you, or preparations you'll enjoy even though they include foods you never particularly cared for before. David has always avoided any dish prepared with eggplant. He has found, however, a recipe he enjoys so much that he's in the kitchen cooking it up, himself. That recipe, by the way, is Eggplant Casserole with Wine on page 268. The idea is to keep an open mind as you change some of the old habits and try some of the different approaches to eating you'll find in these pages. As you do, you will become familiar, as well, with the methodology utilized in defining those foods that will become staples for you and those that you will voluntarily avoid.

Do not be afraid of substitutions like some of the myriad fat-free products that have appeared on the grocery shelves. You may have tried one or two and they taste different, and some are not at all similar to the products they are trying to emulate. Keep trying different brands. The manufacturer of one product that's great may have another that falls short of your expectations and yet the story may be reversed when trying out another manufacturer's substitutes. I've got one case in mind where the fat-free grated cheese offered by one company was like plastic. In trying another brand I found a cheese (fat-free, of course) that tasted and melted just like the real thing but their cream cheese was tasteless. Share this information with your friends and you may be able to save some of the trial and error.

Let's start at the beginning...with breakfast.

BREAKFAST

Breakfast for so many of us is not a sit-down meal but "grab it on the run." Some days we skip breakfast entirely and opt for a better (or bigger) lunch! No more of that, right? This is the time to use a few organizational skills. Save time in those precious morning minutes by thinking about breakfast for the week when you make up your shopping list.

Breakfast can have as few as zero fat grams or as many as 125 fat grams or more, without going overboard with either one. To keep the fat grams closer to the zero mark, we will look, first, at the old standby...oatmeal. Loaded with fiber and with a quick cooking time (a must in most households on weekdays), a cup of cooked oatmeal has less than 2 grams of fat. Farina, Cream of Wheat and Cream of Rice, have no fat. You say you like your cooked cereal with butter and milk? No problem. There is a marvelous butter-flavored substitute on the market called Molly McButter, which, when sprinkled on hot cereal with a splash or 1/2 cup of nonfat skim milk, will give you a taste and consistency you're used to. Another product that fills the need for butter and can be used in liquid form in cooking is Butter Buds. Butter Buds is not as salty-tasting as Molly McButter. Superb, strong butter flavor that can be sprayed on, at the cost of less than a gram of fat for a 2-1/2 second spray, is Weight Watchers Buttery Spray, Pam Buttery Spray and I Can't Believe It's Not Butter. Ultra Promise is another product made to order for us since it's a fat-free margarine that does the trick, while Smart Beat is available at 2 grams of fat per tablespoon. Compare that to real butter or regular margarine (that has the same fat count as butter), at 11 grams per tablespoon. The "lite" or "low-fat" brands of margarine vary in gram count depending on the choice you make. Be sure and check the serving size. Some slip in a "teaspoon" serving instead of a "tablespoon" and that increases your fat gram count threefold! You will find that some of the very low-fat margarines will separate when used in cooking because of the water content. I've had much better results and much lower gram counts from the substitute products just mentioned. And both Molly McButter, Butter Buds and Weight Watchers Buttery Spray have passed the test when tried by some of my toughest critics who are on the lookout for a "diet" taste. If you like fruit added to your cereal (raisins are great in the cooked variety), go right ahead and add whatever your preference is. There are no fat grams to add for berries or raisins, and only 1 gram for a banana.

How about dry cereal? Add a bit of nonfat milk to Corn Flakes, Rice Krispies, Frosted Flakes or Grape Nuts, and you have no fat. Add the nonfat skim milk to one ounce of Cocoa Puffs, Total or Alpha Bits, and you're consuming only 1 gram of fat. Heartland and Cracklin' Oats run 4 grams per ounce. Add some sugar to the cereal and you have not altered the fat-gram count. An alternative that will give you a high fiber, satisfying breakfast is dried fruit, such as prunes, apricots, raisins, dates and other dried goodies.

There are always fresh fruits or canned fruits to lend a cheerful beginning to the day or try a combination of the two. A piece of fresh fruit or an assortment of dried fruits, in a plastic bag, are easy to munch on in the car on the way to work. Sometimes that's the only time some of us have for that first meal of the day. In fact, while shaving, or putting on your make-up, throw a bagel in the microwave for 45 seconds (if frozen), 30 seconds (if refrigerated), and you can grab it on your way out the door. That bagel that gives you such good-chewing flavor is only 1 gram of fat. Check the jumbo bagels that are now appearing on the shelves. They're bigger...they have more fat. Don't forget about how good the banana can be for eating, without a plate, at only 1 gram of fat. Try a banana, mashed, on a slice of fat-free white or whole wheat bread, sprinkle with a spoon of raisins, fold and eat on the run. Very tasty.

There are a number of breadstuffs that serve as breakfast fare and are probably among the most popular ways to start the day. The English Muffin, like the bagel, has only 1 gram of fat. Add a touch of preserves or apple butter to either one and you've added no fat to your count. Just stay away from the butter or margarine. Cream cheese, an old friend of the bagel, has 10 grams of fat per ounce. The Philadelphia Fat Free Cream Cheese tastes just as good as the original and adds absolutely no fat. Alpine Lace and Healthy Choice are also available in a fat free cream cheese in the dairy counter at your supermarket. If you are dying for the taste of butter on the bread, give it a quick spray with the Weight Watchers Buttery Spray. It will do the trick.

And what about the bran muffin that you see in every coffee shop and even at the airport? Unfortunately, every one of them has a different fat content, from 2 to 25 grams! A solution is...make your own! The Marvelous Carrot Muffin (the recipe follows in the recipe section of this book) has less than 1 gram per muffin and is absolutely delicious! Or try a box-mix and use applesauce instead of shortening when you prepare the muffin mix.

So, you've enjoyed a bowl of fruit cocktail, cereal with a sliced banana, a bagel with fat free cream cheese and raspberry preserves, and a fresh cup of coffee (black or with nonfat skim milk and, maybe, some sugar). You might even have thrown in a Marvelous Carrot Muffin for munching on with your second cup of coffee. Your total fat count for breakfast is only 3 to 4 grams. Your neighbor, who remains unenlightened, has just consumed a three-egg cheese omelet, three 2-ounce link sausages, a half-cup of hashed brown potatoes, two biscuits with a slab of butter (the real thing), and a cup of coffee with a dash of coffee cream. He has just totaled 125 to 150 grams of fat! And all he's eaten so far is breakfast!

While the neighbor is trying to stay alert through the morning, you're cooking on complex carbohydrates that supply sustained energy and at about mid-morning you're ready for a little nibble-nourish.

Right on, you say. What can a person, who is changing a lifetime of eating habits, nosh on during a morning break?

MID-MORNING OR ANYTIME SNACK

Carole, who is working on losing 30 pounds, enjoys a half-cup of oatmeal that she microwaves at the office during her mid-morning snack. She throws a few raisins in it on occasion, for variety, and a satisfying sweet taste. During summertime, grapes and a refreshing piece of fruit fill the bill. Linda prefers air-popped popcorn at break time, tossed with a couple, maybe three hits with Weight Watchers Buttery Spray and a shake or two of salt. A touch of heaven, she says, at about 2 grams of fat for the bowl. The bowl contains about six to eight cups. The "lite" popcorn on the market is about 3 grams of fat for three cups. It is a far better choice than the original microwave popcorn, but not as good as the air-popped. We've decided that the air-popped, with a couple to three seconds of Buttery Spray, tastes better, too. Could that be because we know how many fat grams we've avoided consuming? Or is it because of the even coverage of the oh-so buttery flavor we get, the low-fat way?

You have no doubt already experienced the difficulty of assuming the mind-set to diet to lose weight, or to follow your doctor's advice to diet to lower cholesterol, when you are faced with the munchies. One of the greatest adjustments to be made when changing eating habits is finding the right morsel to satisfy the in-between hungries. I call it a nibble-nourish but, let's face it, it's a snack, a nosh, a bite, some sort of edible to mitigate the driving force that makes you blow the whole deal and end up with a bag of cashews or a jumbo Milky Way clutched in your tight fist. When the half-pound bag of M&M Peanuts calls to you from the grocer's shelf, it helps to have an alternative in mind so your legs can carry you to a fulfilling alternative. Be prepared!

The following list of goodies includes a variety of substitute snacks that will leave you guilt-free. Any entry on this list adds no more than 1 gram of fat to your daily count, yet the morsels included here have been approved by practiced noshers who know their nibbles.

THE NIBBLE-NOURISH

Raw vegetables with a dip of fat-free sour cream, prepared with dried onion soup mix or granulated vegetable bouillon.

A baked potato (any size) with fat-free sour cream, chives, and 1 tablespoon imitation bacon bits.

A slice of fat-free toast with apple butter.

A banana mashed on fat-free bread with a handful of raisins sprinkled on top.

Air-popped popcorn with a 2-1/2 second spray of Weight Watchers Buttery Spray.

A cup of Wheat Chex sprinkled with Cajun seasoning mix and baked until crisp.

A cup of herb tea stirred with a cinnamon stick.

A skewer of mushrooms, green pepper and onion pieces, grilled.

A Marvelous Carrot Muffin. Recipe on page 349

Two rice cakes spread with orange marmalade.

A fruit skewer with melons and assorted fruit chunks.

A crunchy dill pickle.

A glass of Bloody Mary Mix with a stalk of celery.

A slice of fat-free bread, fat-free mayonnaise with 2 teaspoons grated Parmesan cheese sprinkled on top and broiled until bubbling.

A handful of carrot slices.

5 flavored mini rice cakes.

Fresh apple chunks flavored with cinnamon.

A cup of Old El Paso Mexe-beans mixed with rice.

A Dole frozen Fruit & Juice Bar.

2 fat-free Fig Newtons.

A cup of Campbell's Tomato Soup prepared with water or nonfat skim milk.

A pita pocket filled with steamed vegetables with a dollop of fat-free Thousand Island Dressing.

1/2 cup of fat-free ice cream or fat-free yogurt.

A baked potato with Old El Paso Thick & Chunky Salsa.

A cup of pasta tossed with 2 tablespoons of the Basic Marinara Sauce. Recipe on page 226.

A cup of applesauce sprinkled with cinnamon.

A toasted English Muffin with strawberry jam.

A toasted English Muffin with fat-free cheese melted on top.

An Archway Fat-Free Oatmeal Raisin Cookie.

A small bowl of salad stuff with fat-free dressing.

1/2 cup of raisins or dates.

2 tablespoons of tuna salad prepared with fat-free mayonnaise and chopped celery on melba toast.

A handful of Mr. Phipps Fat-Free Pretzel Chips with 2 tablespoons of Bari's Clam Dip. Recipe on page 111.

A toasted or heated cinnamon bagel.

4 ounces of club soda mixed with 4 ounces of fruit juice.

4 Entenmann's Fat Free Oatmeal Chocolatey Chip Cookies.

A fat-free tortilla (corn or flour) wrapped around a mixture of Quick Chili Beans (recipe on page 204) and Red Rice (recipe on page 224) with salsa.

5 pieces Teddy Grahams.

An English Muffin spread with tomato sauce, green peppers and mushroom slices and baked.

Sugar free bubble gum.

A slice of fat-free pound cake spread with blueberry preserves.

Half a grapefruit and an orange, sectioned and combined with a dash of honey.

A Special K Eggo Waffle with fat-free ice cream.

A fat-free corn tortilla in triangles, toasted and dipped in salsa.

A frozen banana.

3 fat-free old-fashioned sourdough pretzels.

Healthy Choice Fat Free Chile Con Queso cheese dip with toasted fat-free corn tortillas. Recipe on page 112.

A Health Valley Fat-Free Granola Bar.

A Hostess Crumb Cake.

SnackWell's Cinnamon Graham Snacks.

There you have the beginning of a nibbler's answer to low-fat or no-fat noshing. You will think of others as you become more familiar with fat-gram counting, and you'll find additional foods that can fill in as snacks in the HORS D'OEUVRE category of the recipe section. You'll be gratified by the new products being introduced in your supermarket everyday that you'll be able to add to your repertoire.

LUNCH

Lunch is a bit more complicated. You have restaurants and other people to contend with. Concerning "other people" there are two ways you can handle your new lifestyle. The first way is to make a point of telling anyone who will listen to you exactly what you're up to and how you're doing. That way you will have the support of those who are naturally supportive and positive, or the ridicule of those who are naturally skeptical and negative. Of course, you can always use these negative reactions to your benefit by a determined effort to "show them!" However, on the other hand, if you do want to keep things quiet until you've become accustomed to this new life, it can be done. Then you'll have the gratification of being asked, "What have you done? You look so good! Have you lost weight?"

See how the foods you most often eat for lunch fit on the fat meter and make some adjustments to make them work for you. Let's see if the lunch plans we make here fit you.

This can be really simple. Salads are great. They are easy to find in almost every restaurant and require adherence to just a few guidelines to keep you within your fat quotient. Stay away from the mayonnaise-based group on the salad bar. The bean and pasta salads usually have added oils, which you can't measure, and therefore can't count. Everything else is fair game since fresh vegetables and beans (like those garbanzo or red kidney beans) have no fat at all, or only traces, which do not need to be counted. If, however, avocado (or guacamole) is on the salad bar, skip it. There are 33 grams of fat in one medium avocado!

When visiting a salad bar, look for the low calorie dressings that so many restaurants now carry. These offer about 3 to 5 grams of fat per tablespoon. A couple of teaspoons (there are 3 in a tablespoon), with a bit of additional vinegar (usually placed with a cruet of oil near the dressings), should dress your salad in style. Or, you can use the trick my daughter, Bari, taught me: an easy way to give your taste buds a treat. Place the dressing on the side of your plate or on another small plate. Dip your fork tines in the dressing and take a forkful of salad. You'd be amazed at how full the flavor of the dressing is in your mouth, while confining the amount, for the whole salad consumed, to about one teaspoon. At the same time, the salad doesn't get limp or soggy. It works! A teaspoon of regular salad dressing runs about 2 to 3 grams of fat.

Stay away from the bread or breadsticks. Unless you have a gram count on the bread, you can be fooled. Ask for crackers, instead. Melba toast, plain, is fat free; if wheat, it contains only 1 gram for three crackers. Saltines have a mere 1 to 2 grams in 5 to seven crackers and Waverly Wafers have 3 grams in four crackers. Most of the crackers served to you will be a brand you recognize and your fat counter will recognize it, too.

Then, of course, there are those days you're joining someone for lunch who loves the TGIF or Bennigan type restaurants, the kind of place that has a menu of 15 pages with everything from fried potato skins to nachos, fried jumbo shrimp to chicken quesadillas. These restaurants are not as big a problem as one might think. Look for veggies. They are prepared steamed as an alternative to salad. Some soy sauce at the table adds flavor, or, you can ask for stir-fried veggies prepared with very little oil. You'd be surprised how accommodating your server can be.

And stir-fry brings us to a happy solution to the "where should we go for lunch?" dilemma. Suggest Chinese or Japanese! Prepared with the facts, any of the Oriental food places are a gold mine for people who eat wisely and don't confine themselves to food prepared only at home. The facts I refer to are spelled out in frightening detail in an article which appeared in *Nutrition Action Health Letter*, September, 1993, published by the Center For Science In The Public Interest. These good people conducted a study of Chinese food from a variety of restaurants in Washington, D.C., San Francisco and Chicago. The fat grams in some of the favorites would supply more than three days' worth of your fat intake. CSPI shows 4 cups of House Fried Rice has 50 grams of fat, Sweet and Sour Pork has 71, House Lo Mein has 36 and 1 Egg Roll has 11! Yet eating Chinese food wisely is no different from any other kind of good-tasting restaurant meal, in that you don't have to deny yourself if you choose wisely and adjust your approach.

Look carefully at the menu. Avert your eyes from the beef and pork. You'll find a vast array of seafood and poultry designed to taste divine and keep you happy while you're eating healthy. Order stir-fried vegetables and ask them to go easy on the oil. Better yet, order the vegetables steamed and ask for the sauce on the side. The vegetable chop suey, broccoli in hot garlic sauce, green beans in Szechuan sauce, or any of these type dishes with steamed rice are very flavorful. If served in the sauce, the trick here is to place a small amount of rice to the side of your plate and tap the veggies gently to remove any excess sauce. Be sure to order extra rice. You want to eat this food like the Orientals do: lots of rice with the saucy foods to act as the flavor. With plenty of rice you'll eat only half as much of the dish, thereby cutting the fat gram count in half. The sauce left on the vegetables is delicious and when eaten with the remainder of the rice is a filling, satisfying lunch. The fat gram count remains light. I usually consider a lunch like the kind I just described at about 5 to 6 fat grams. Enjoy a lunch like this and use this approximate number and you'll have no problem staying within your limit for the day. And, what joy! The fortune cookie has no fat at all!

Just recently a friend and I were at a favorite Chinese place and she ordered the Lo Mein. She requested it be prepared with broccoli, onions and very little oil. She was overjoyed with the flavor and probably ended up with about 6 grams of fat in her lunch.

A wonderful place for lunch is the Japanese restaurant where the food is prepared on a grill right in front of you. They can stir-fry for you using no more than a teaspoon of oil. That meal is about 5 grams of fat, depending on the meat, if any, you choose to go with the veggies. Go for the steamed rice, not fried, and skip the little fried noodles. They add up to 11 grams per cup!

Remember that the Oriental countries, as you read about earlier in this book, enjoy a much lower rate of heart disease and fat-caused cancers. The diet, however, that can be attributed to these findings is different from the Americanized version. We use much more oil in preparation and add more meats. These dishes in their original form are served with rice as the food and the meats as condiments. Most Americans consume a much greater amount of protein than the body requires. Be comfortable in your use of rice, a complex carbohydrate. Beware of the egg roll! Skip the tempura!

Think about some of the restaurants most frequented by the people you lunch with. Work out beforehand the foods that will most easily fit your lifestyle and when you get there you won't have to search, frantically, for something on the menu that will please you and also fit the fat measure. And don't let your friends intimidate you. They are concerned because you're not eating the fried chicken or the hamburger, and they try to convince you it won't hurt to "eat it just this once." Keep in mind they mean well, and then ignore them and order what you want! A good solution for this situation is a baked potato (just about every American-style restaurant offers one), dry, to which you add a tablespoon of sour cream (2 1/2 grams of fat), and since salsa is becoming as popular as ketchup, ask for some salsa and put a tablespoon or more on top of the sour cream! The salsa is, most often, free of any fat and it gives the potato a fantastic, bright flavor. Add a salad, dry, with the dressing on the side. Almost all salad dressings have about 6 to 8 grams of fat per tablespoon. By eating the salad with the fork-tines trick, only a teaspoon or less is consumed. Add the 2 1/2 grams for the sour cream and 1 gram for a few saltines to the 2 1/2, or so, for the dressing and you have a total of about 6 grams of fat for lunch. If the restaurant serves a really good Mexican salsa, a dollop of that instead of the sour cream and you've cut the fat grams of this lunch down to about 3 1/2.

Another approach is the broiled shrimp (request that no butter be used to brush the shrimp) at about 1 gram for six jumbo prawns, and have the baked potato on the side. If you throw in the vegetable of the day, you have a total of about 4 to 5 grams, and that includes a touch of butter or oil with which the veggie was prepared in the kitchen. This, obviously, can be a super dinner out, as well. And how can your friends feel sorry for you? Or you feel sorry for you, for that matter! Feel sorry, instead, for your friends with their fat-soaked diets!

How about that steak joint that's always been a favorite of the gang for lunch? How do you say, "no," or ruin everyone's time? You don't! You say, "yes," but order a bit differently. Have the grilled or steamed shrimp, and the salad bar, utilizing some of the tricks we talked about. Or, how about this? If there is barbecued or baked beans on the menu, try an order on the baked potato. Fabulous taste, a different approach! With a salad on the side, it's heaven.

Once you start thinking "grams" and begin recognizing the right stuff, the rest is easy! Again, it helps to ask for consideration on butters and add-ons like cheese. The kitchen is usually happy to leave them off for you, if you make the request. And our requests are rapidly becoming more commonplace.

The sandwich, an American institution, is a difficult lunch to fit into any diet...except this one! Not too long ago, Phil, just starting out with this lifestyle, said his greatest problem was not having the freedom to take a sandwich to the office for lunch. He said, "I can stand any diet if I can have a normal lunch. And to me a normal lunch is a sandwich that I can eat at my desk." This happy weight-loser is eating a tuna or turkey salad sandwich at his desk, racking up only 2 grams of fat for lunch! The salad is prepared with Kraft's or Smart Beat Free Mayonnaise, celery and lemon juice, and a touch of pickle relish, on two slices of fat-free whole wheat or white bread, with lettuce, tomato and a slab of fat-free mayo on the bread. Chicken salad, on the other hand, will add about 4 grams of fat to his day, using about four ounces of chicken. Where does he find his fat-free bread? At the supermarket, when he's choosing the bread for the week, he reads the labels and finds those that are fat free, one of which is Wonder Bread. Safeway also makes a fat-free loaf. You can find a wonderful French bread in the refrigerator section made by Pillsbury. They call it "Crusty French Loaf" and it pops out of the tube for fresh baking. The fat gram count is slightly more than zero per 1 inch slice.

Columbo's Fat Free Sour Dough Bread is another gem you'll find in loaves and rolls on the supermarket shelves. There are so many available, with more brands joining the fat-free bandwagon every day. Check your supermarket shelves for those carried by your individual market.

Don't forget the wonderful world of pita bread when thinking "sandwich." Check the product nutrition information for the fat gram count of the different brands. They do vary. Make a junior stir-fry of onion, green bell pepper, celery and mushrooms, sliced and sautéed in a touch of chicken stock (defatted, of course). Heat up a pita and stick this veggie delight into the pocket and chow down. You can add some garlic powder to the stir-fry pan, or some tomato, maybe even a teaspoon or two of Basic Marinara Sauce (page 226), for a tasty zip. The variations can be delectable and are confined only to the limits of your imagination! If you are at the office, take vegetables you've cooked the night before, heat the veggies in the microwave and set aside. Stick the pita in the microwave for 30 seconds. It will be soft, fresh tasting and perfect for stuffing.

There are a number of other "easy to prepare" lunches that will make you forget that you are "staying healthy." When you have some good leftovers from dinner, freeze them in lunch-size servings. If you haven't used a microwaveable plastic bag, run the bag under hot water. The block of frozen food will slide out of the bag. You can thaw it out in the microwave and heat it through in very little time, enjoying a delicious meal in minutes.

Baked potatoes are great, too. After washing and pricking with a fork, these little beauties microwave in about ten minutes. Turn after 5 minutes on high, microwave for 3 more minutes and stick a fork in the potato to test for softness. If necessary, microwave an additional 2 to 3 minutes. Add some Molly McButter, if you like, fat-free sour cream and Baco's, which contain only 1 gram per tablespoon. The size of the potato will not affect your gram count because it is free of fat. You can use salsa to add some spice to the potato, or, as an alternative, try fat-free shredded cheddar, sour cream and salsa for a potato nacho-style.

Another super potato lunch is a Restuffed Potato prepared at home and reheated in the office. These potato treats can be frozen and thawed out in the microwave or in the fridge overnight. The recipe is on page 278.

Eating lunch you've prepared yourself puts you in control, and, in the beginning, you may want to go this route. It won't take long before you get used to finding the foods you enjoy that are low-fat or no-fat when you are ready to order from the offerings of your favorite restaurants. Remember, the idea is not to feel deprived, because as you can see, there are inviting choices you can make from almost any menu. Just remember to remain in charge and not allow a server or friends to intimidate you.

I was in a well-known D.C. restaurant recently with a dear friend who eats the way you will soon be eating. Kathy requested a red sauce on her pasta, which she knew was lower in fat grams than the olive oil and garlic pasta. The server very graciously informed Kathy that he was sure that this was not possible. She then requested, even more graciously, that he check with the kitchen since she felt sure they would not mind doing this for her. She smiled. He smiled. He returned seven minutes later with her order and presented her red sauce with a flourish. He smiled. She smiled.

As you can see, there are many approaches to a satisfying lunch without making those with whom you are eating feel sorry for you, or sorry for themselves for eating with you. You can actually carry this off without anyone knowing you're tallying fat grams.

AFTERNOON SNACK

Don't forget, you still have an afternoon nibble-nourish to help you get through to dinner without an overwhelming desire to eat the table! Now is an exceptionally good time for some fat-free cookies, or perhaps a handful or two of pretzels. Refer to page 44 where you will find a long list of goodies for both morning and afternoon nibbling. The carrot slices or fruit slices work well here, too. I've turned to one of the favorites, home-baked muffins, when confronted with a raging sweet tooth at mid-afternoon, and it works! Flavored mini rice cakes are sweet and crunchy, a prerequisite for a satisfying snack, at only 1 gram for 5 cakes. And if you haven't done the popcorn yet, it's a natural. Some applesauce, sprinkled with cinnamon, is a refreshing pleasure. If you're into a snack with some kick...a crunchy dill pickle is a mouthful. Given some time you will add your own 1-gram nibbles to the list. You'll get a feel for the kind of snack that fits you, and your day, best. The same rule for variety applies here, as it does with your meals. Enjoy changes in your snacks so you don't become bored and run out for a "harmless" bag of corn chips.

DINNER

By the time you get to the dinner table you've tallied up about 5 to 12 grams of fat in the day. When you were on those calorie-counting diets, dinner time was a tremendous worry or a terribly boring handful of carrot sticks. The "sensible" dinner! 3 ounces of meat, a vegetable, and a salad with lemon juice. No pasta, no potato, no beans, no rice. And, certainly, no bread!

Take heart! With this lifestyle, this is the best time of the day. Oh, yes, I can imagine that look of disbelief on your face. So far you haven't seen "exciting" in these suggested meals. Just hang in there.

The recipes that follow can enhance your table. And there is no reason why some of your old favorites cannot be adapted to a lower-fat fare. There are just a few recipes that call for more exotic ingredients than those you already have on your pantry shelf right now. You will find these in the Oriental food market or in the foreign food aisle at your supermarket. These dishes are so delicious and satisfying that they've been served to innocent guests who eat with great gusto, never knowing they've been duped into eating a healthy dinner. Yes, we have friends who believe, "If it's good for you and especially, if it's low in fat, it CANNOT taste good!" Even dessert can be wickedly good and, for those who must feel they've cheated, dessert can taste so good they'll think they had.

Let's look at some of the dinner favorites and see where we stand in the fat count. Four large shrimp contain about 1/2 gram, boiled, broiled or steamed. Four ounces of fresh yellowfin tuna fish contain 1 gram. Molly McButter and lemon juice KEEP the count at 1 gram. Canned in water, tuna has only 1 gram for two ounces. Chicken breast, broiled, without the skin, has 4.6 grams for four ounces; dark meat, however, has 9.9 grams! Turkey breast, roasted without the skin, has less than 1 gram per ounce; butter-basted turkey (such as Butterball brand), 3 grams per ounce. Chicken frankfurter, 11 grams; a turkey frankfurter, 8 grams; a turkey patty, 5 grams. Obviously, additional fat has been added to the turkey patties and franks to increase the grams per ounce, as shown. This is an example of the importance of reading the label and finding products in your counter book.

What about beef and pork? Here are some numbers for you: four ounces of flank steak (we're talking about the size of a deck of cards), lean and braised, 15 grams; three ounces of ground beef, extra-lean, broiled, 14 grams; canned corned beef hash, eight ounces, over 25 grams; pork loin, blade, lean (fat trimmed), one chop, broiled, three and one-half ounces, 12.7 grams. You can see why beef and pork are not on my most-wanted list! You'll see no recipes including red meat in this book. If you choose to use some red meats in your dishes, try to do as the Orientals do and use it as a condiment, for flavoring, rather than as the main food.

At this juncture you are wondering how I am going to take the evening meal and reduce it to a low-fat phenomenon that you will actually enjoy and then prepare again at another time. The test for us has always been that second go-round with a recipe. When we prepare a new dish, spend the time in the kitchen following the instructions and then sit down with the expectant taste buds primed, and nod to each other and say, "Mmmm, not bad," we know the final decision has not yet been determined. Three weeks later, if one of us asks, "Shall we do that dish with the eggplant, again?" It's a never-to-make-the-grade recipe if the response is, "Nah, lets do the other eggplant...with the potatoes." The answer is not to eat because it's good for you, but to eat because it feels good. And this criterion does not change merely because your health and, therefore, your approach to a healthier diet has become more important. Let's face it, if you want to continue eating "right" for your health's sake, it must pass the "feels-good" test or the determination to make the changes falters. Then you're right back to the old way of eating that does make you feel good.

The suggestions for your evening meal that follow in the next pages are all within the parameters of your new 20-gram lifestyle. I feel confident you'll find a number of dishes that remind you of what you considered to be a part of the "good old days," when it comes to your eating habits, and yet they fit in, comfortably, when prepared correctly. And the preparations can be found in the recipe section of this book.

Have you ever had a dinner that starts off with a creamy spinach dip, crackers, and assorted hors d'oeuvres, roast turkey, mashed potatoes with thick mushroom gravy, vegetables enhanced with a fine buttery flavor, bread and dessert...on a diet? Or, better yet, a heaping plate of pasta with a spicy marinara sauce, loaded with mushrooms, maybe shrimp and clams in the sauce, and along with the salad, served in a creamy Italian dressing, a couple of hunks of crispy sourdough bread? Perhaps you would prefer a huge stir-fry with chicken or shrimp, green bell peppers and onions, or mixed vegetables in a hot Szechuan sauce over steamed rice?

How about a salad of assorted lettuces, carrots, cucumber, celery, radish, artichoke hearts, pickled beets, red kidney beans, peas, mushrooms, some red cabbage for color (have we left anything out? Oh, yes, Bermuda onion!) with tuna or tuna salad, or turkey breast slices. Think of all the wonderful things you like to include in your salad at the most extensive salad bar in history. Just leave out the red meats and use the fat-free mayo. Use your imagination on this one. An easy way to expand your selection of salad stuffs is to look at the veggies in the frozen food section at your supermarket. Any of these can be run under cold water for two or three minutes, or steamed in the microwave for a minute, so that they're crunchy and fresh-tasting. Think of broccoli or lima beans, peas or corn, which are available in the big, value-priced, plastic bags. You can toss them in a colander, run cold water over them until they are thawed, throw them in the salad makings and thereby change the personality of the salad to keep the variety interesting and exciting.

Change your choice of salad dressings, too. You'll find some recipes in this book and you'll find a vast assortment of fat-free dressings at the friendly corner market. These can be the fat-free variety or the low-fat, from which you will discard some of the oil and add vinegar or water. Keep a measure of what you're removing from the contents of the bottle and figure your fat grams from the label with the appropriate deduction, all the while keeping in mind, a tablespoon of oil contains 14 fat grams. Also, remember to check the manufacturer's estimation of a serving size.

The salad course is a natural, whether you opt for a tossed salad with a choice of dressings served, or the Antipasto, with, perhaps, a platter of Cucumber Salad (page 127). Selections for the salad course can be found in the salad section of the recipes, following, and using the fat-free dressings you prepare from this book or purchase at the supermarket, you'll have no problem adapting some of your own favorites.

You'd prefer more hot dinner ideas? Okay! You can always opt for chicken breast smothered in mushroom-wine sauce, flavored with garlic and oregano, served with a Restuffed

Potato (page 278), along with asparagus with a light butter flavor or fresh, steamed spinach with a hint of olive oil and garlic.

Is your mouth watering yet? Well, then, let's not stop here!

How about the simple, yet elegant dinner of broiled, fresh fish or shellfish? The vegetables tossed in a light tarragon sauce, with sage-flavored potatoes and a serving of crunchy cole slaw. Of course, after a hard day's work you want a dinner easy to prepare, you say. On the weekend prepare a pot of Alaskan Three-Bean Soup (page 169) or Aunt Rose's Minestrone (page 172). Reheat upon returning home after a long day, while a loaf of seeded rye bread or a couple of pita breads are warming in the oven. Another surefire satisfier is a bowl of Bahamian Fish Chowder (page 189) or Fish Stew (page 337). These, too, can be prepared beforehand, and taste even better after being refrigerated and then reheated.

Speaking of soups, these can be simple and really filling. A big bowl of hot soup with a sandwich or a hunk of hot, crusty bread can be nurturing and the answer to your prayers when all you want to do is put your feet up and relax after a tough day. Do try to stay away from any creamed soups. Again, check the fat grams and that will guide you. Let's say you've chosen Progresso Healthy Classics Lentil Soup at 1 gram for eight ounces, or Campbell's Condensed Tomato Soup with 2 grams for eight ounces. Heat up 1/2 to 3/4 cup rice (use brown rice if you want a chewier consistency and the benefits of the healthy bran), place in the bowl and add the hot soup. You've just made a bowl of soup into a meal! If you have room in your fat count, have two! There are a number of soups you can fill out this way. A helpful trick with a great many canned soups is to store the can in the refrigerator for four hours or more before opening. The fat will congeal on the top making it easy for you to remove. You won't affect the flavor but you'll make a dent in the fat gram count.

It's easy to find soups that are robust and taste so good that you cannot remember that you are, in fact, "watching what you eat!"

Now that we've covered a few ways of satisfying the week-day hungries without falling overboard or losing your way, and still maintaining a happy, full tummy, how about the tough times? How do you handle the preparation of a sumptuous dinner for guests? You are in the driver's seat here. You are preparing the dinner which must be, absolutely, the last word in mouth-watering perfection. There is no concern about hurting the feelings of the host or hostess because of the high-fat foods served and the conflict between eating or abstaining. You are the chef extraordinaire. You are going to present to your guests a smashing, bang-up dinner and they will never know how kind to their bodies you've been unless you brag to them about it after dessert. For heaven sakes, wait until after dessert!

Playing with this dinner a bit, you'll find making the changes you'd like or varying the presentation for different dinners, will be a snap. By all means, start off with a few hors d'oeuvres. How about Salmon Pate Triangles, Cucumber Turkey Spread, Crab Curry Spread (pages 94, 105 and 91) with toasted bread rounds or melba rounds. You could always go with the South of the Border flavor of Bean and Cheese Nachos (page 114). When a suitable amount of time has been enjoyed in entertaining conversation, and the state of politics and the economy of the nation has been thoroughly examined, it's time to adjourn to the dinner table.

A popular appetizer is shrimp cocktail with Spicy Cocktail Sauce (page 147). Of course, you may want to serve both the red sauce and a Remoulade Sauce (page 146) as well. Crab can substitute for the shrimp, or you may want to start with the Fruit Salad (page 121). This may be followed by a soup. You could serve the French Potato Soup (page 178) which doubles as Vichyssoise when cold, or go for a heartier soup: Meredith's Minestrone (page 173).

The salad course is a natural, whether you opt for a tossed salad with a choice of dressings served, or the Antipasto (page 117), with, perhaps, a platter of Cucumber and Onions.

A fruity sorbet is elegant served at this point, to clear the palate. It gives the table an opportunity to take a breather between courses and the chef a chance to get the entree ready to serve. A wonderful advantage of this touch of class is the sorbet contains no fat. Check the frozen dessert section at the supermarket or prepare it yourself (page 343).

If you are going for an Italian flavor, Simple Spinach Lentil Lasagna (page 231) is a great do-ahead, which merely needs reheating for serving and leaves you more time to relax with your guests. Another goody for do-ahead is Chicken-Sghetti (page 287). The sauce is prepared the day before, allowing the flavors to meld. The spaghetti can be cooked ahead, too, and all you need to do is run hot water over the pasta in the colander to heat it up for serving. Then spoon the heated sauce on top and serve with freshly-grated Parmesan cheese or fat-free Parmesan served in a bowl with a spoon so your guests don't see the fat-free label. Have crispy breadsticks stuffed in tumblers on the table along with Columbo's Fat Free Sourdough bread, baked hot and crusty. Mama mia, that's good eating.

You were thinking of more Continental cuisine? How about Chicken Breast Marsala (page 288), with Green Rice (page 221) and Green Beans with Mushrooms (page 258). The Baked Herbed Fish (page 333) is a dish fit for the company table, as is Sole or Flounder with Capers (page 336), either one served with Parsley Potato Patties (page 280) and Zucchini Cheese Bake (page 253). Fat-free dinner rolls round out this entree.

You have just served five palate-pleasing courses of gourmet caliber, and, depending on which entree you've chosen to prepare, total fat grams amount to approximately 10 to 12 per serving, well within your daily schedule. Since you've known what you were serving for dinner you adjusted your breakfast, lunch and nibbles to accommodate a loaded evening meal. But, I'm sure you've noticed, we haven't talked dessert yet! We know this has to be special.

Dessert can be an assortment of fresh, ripe berries, fresh fruits or try fresh pineapple slices, grapes, dates and apple, skewered. This is aesthetically pleasing and tastes good, too.

Sounds too much like diet fare, you say? Okay. Let's go for broke! There is some doubt there will be a guest ready for a rich dessert, but you can certainly go for the fruit skewers along with the following: fat-free slices of pound cake covered with Sealtest Vanilla-Fudge fat-free ice cream or Entenmann's Fat-Free Chocolate Cake with a scoop of fat-free vanilla ice cream. How about Healthy Choice Praline and Caramel Premium Low Fat Ice Cream (tastes like the fat-laden ice cream to me!) or Fudge Brownie Premium Low Fat Ice Cream, each with 2 grams of fat per four ounce serving, with cookies that are fat-free from Health Valley or Entenmann's. Check the other fat-free delicacies on your grocer's shelves. You will be surprised by the divine cakes and pastries with the fat-free label, and more are added each day. Add a pot of freshly-brewed coffee and you've served a seven-course dinner, fit for the most elegant table, at a grand total of 15, or so, fat grams per person. Aren't you proud of yourself? And your guests never would have believed that this scrumptious dinner was so healthy.

If this company dinner you're planning is informal and you're looking for some fun foods to offer a change of pace, and at the same time satisfy the need for robust good eating, try this touch of Mexico. Along with salsa and your favorite brand of baked corn chips or baked pita bread, serve Bean Dip (page 113) and Chili Con Queso (page 112). Openers can be a salad prepared with assorted lettuces (romaine, radicchio and head lettuce), tomatoes (chopped rather than sliced), celery, carrots, green bell pepper, red beans, corn kernels, and a few ounces of melted Healthy Choice Fat Free Grated Cheddar Cheese tossed in for flavor and color. Serve some fat-free Italian or WishBone Lite Classic Dijon Vinaigrette from which you've removed about ninety-five percent of the oil and to which you've added Red Wine Vinegar for added kick. Follow the salad with a huge bowl of simmering David's Famous Chili (page 304) served with Red Rice (page 224), fat-free steaming flour or corn tortillas (steam them in Saran Wrap for one minute in the microwave), grated fat-free cheddar and Monterey Jack cheeses, with some salsa (Old El Paso makes a thick and chunky in mild, medium or hot that is out of sight and has no added oil) and a side of fat-free sour cream (served in a little bowl so no one knows!) and jalapeño pepper slices. Everyone takes or makes their own dinner. It works and it tastes so good!

What about going to someone else's home for dinner and you don't want to dictate requirements to them? You can handle this in one simple way. Choose to nibble abundantly at home beforehand. You have at home all the low and no-fat foods on which to become somewhat satiated before entering a world of unknowns.

Your host or hostess will not be offended if you are a light eater avoiding the fat-filled dips and chips (10 grams per ounce) and peanuts (13 grams per ounce) and go for the pretzels, if they've been served, at 1 gram per ounce.

Certainly look for those foods served that fit your lifestyle at the hors d'oeuvres table. The problem does become stickier at the dinner table. Use good judgment. Heavy on the steamed vegetables, lots of salad while skimpy on the dressing. It's possible to move aside heavy gravies and cream sauces, without being obvious, and thereby save gobs of fat. Just be aware.

You have survived an evening at Kathleen's and her fabulous kitchen. She's renowned for her style and serving grace. Her preparation of exquisite cuisine is revered and irresistible. You know you fought the good fight and probably went over your 20 gram limit. Maybe a little, maybe a lot. The following day you return to your normal lifestyle, not giving the previous evening a moment's remorse. This momentary fall from grace is simply that: momentary. By returning to your own regimen, without a bout of punishment and exaggerated denial, you will avoid an unhealthy binge-starve cycle. Since one evening's indiscretion will not reverse all you've accomplished, be good to yourself! Just carry on!

CHAPTER VII

TRICKS & TREATS

How do you maintain the ethnicity of some of those foods that are old favorites yet do not appear among the recipes that follow? You are, of course, going to want to prepare some special dishes with just a change here, and an adjustment there, to make them fit your low-fat requirements. This can be accomplished with a little test-kitchen analysis, ingenuity and simple logic.

Take some of your favorite recipes and do a little whittling.

You know that using lots of meat adds lots of fat. If the recipe calls for ground beef or pork, use ground turkey and drain well after browning. If you have lots of time, rinse the drained turkey, reserving the liquid. Refrigerate the meat. Place the liquid in the freezer for about a half-hour and when the fat has congealed on top, remove the fat and return as much of the stock as you need to enhance the dish. Trim all fat from any meats when you must use the meat for flavor, and be sure to drain where possible. Reduce the amount of meat in the dish to enhance the flavor, more as a condiment than as the main feature. If the dish can be refrigerated before serving or reheating to serve, be sure to refrigerate for at least four hours to facilitate removal of any fat that has congealed on top. Trim any skin or fat from poultry before cooking. Removing the fat after cooking allows seepage of the fat into the meat, even though you cannot detect it. For this reason fried chicken is not on the list of accepted foods. Removing the fried skin still leaves too much of the fat in the chicken meat. Try to use the white meat of the poultry instead of the dark.

If cheese is called for, use a low-fat or no-fat cheese. Remember to check your supermarket for Healthy Choice Nonfat Grated Cheese for really good flavor and melting capabilities. You'll find some imitation cheeses react more like plastic than the kind of meltable cheese you're looking for. Borden's is one of the tastiest of the cheese slices in the fat-free genre for use in sandwiches. If you use low-fat, instead of fat-free cheese, try grating the cheese. It gives you much more bang for the buck. A little grated cheese goes much farther, and a good deal less is required for topping or seasoning. Egg substitutes can be used instead of whole eggs, or use two egg whites to replace one whole egg, to avoid the 5 to 7 grams of fat in the yolk. Different recipes may call for a slight adjustment in the substitution.

Analyze your dessert recipes and see if substitutions and slight changes can be made to render them lower in fat or fat-free. In addition to using egg substitutes you will find that using crushed pineapple or applesauce, as a substitute for oil or shortening, will work in cake and cupcake recipes.

In certain entrees try the recipe without meat entirely, using additional vegetables, beans, bouillon or defatted stock. A successful application of this technique is our Spinach Lasagna Roll-Ups (page 229) which was originally based on ground beef with the spinach as the optional ingredient. We found the beef to be the optional ingredient and opted to do without it. At first the dish was prepared with ground turkey to sub for the beef. Served numerous times to guests who would have turned up their noses at anything but the original, we received demands for seconds, and sometimes, thirds! What turned out to be especially gratifying was the same response when the ground turkey was left out, too. Cooked with spinach alone the dish is superb with salad and hot crusty French bread. You certainly don't miss the meat.

The majority of recipes you will find in books and newspapers call for anywhere from 1 tablespoon to 1/2 cup oil for sautéing. Whether it be olive, vegetable, peanut, canola, corn, safflower or sesame...oil is oil. Oil is fat. A tablespoon of oil is 14 grams of fat. A teaspoon is 4 2/3 grams. A spray-on oil (Pam, Olive Oil Flavored Pam, Mazola, Wesson, Weight Watchers Buttery Spray) is 1 gram of fat per each two and one-half second spray. These figures make a very good case for sautéing in something other than oil, and utilizing spray-on oil as an attractive alternative when flavors must be enhanced with a touch of butter (Weight Watchers Buttery Spray) or olive oil (Pam). The usage is simple.

Sautéing onions, garlic and seasonings is one of the most common methods for starting sauces, soups, stir-fry and casseroles. There are two easy ways to accomplish sautéing sans oil: stove-top and microwave.

Stove-top, you can use a bit of wine, either white or red. The alcohol content will cook off. You may also use bouillon (chicken, beef or vegetable), broth, or fat-free canned broth or defatted stock. The stock is defatted by skimming the fat off the top, following refrigeration. Introduce your liquid to the pan or pot, add the onions, along with other ingredients for sautéing, according to directions, and cook on high, stirring, as you would had you used oil. The oils don't cook away as rapidly as these liquids so be prepared to add more liquid, if necessary. The same method may be used in a wok, stirring during the stir-fry procedure, adding the vegetables as you go and the additional ingredients such as oyster and soy sauces, with the corn starch for thickening, as you would had you started with oil. There will be no noticeable difference in the taste of the dish. When sesame oil is an ingredient it is usually part of the recipe for flavor rather than sautéing. The recommended amount of this oil can be reduced to impart the necessary flavor enhancement, while reducing the fat count.

Try using the microwave for fat-free sautéing. Using the proper microwave-proof container cook the vegetables with a small amount of water, broth or defatted stock on the highest setting until the desired affect is achieved. Continue, then, with the rest of the recipe.

These methods of sautéing can be used with just about every recipe calling for a softened vegetable. There are times, however, when you want to braise or sear a food, such as the chicken breasts in the recipe for Chicken Breasts in White Wine and Mushrooms. In this situation, Olive Oil Flavored Pam is perfect, sprayed on the bottom of a very hot pan, adding only 1 to 2 grams of fat to the recipe. The high heat of the pan seals in the juices and the olive oil flavor is a perfect enhancement for the wine and mushrooms.

The Weight Watchers Buttery Spray, as mentioned before, is the answer to low-fat, buttery popcorn that tastes absolutely sinful and the spray gives much more even coverage than the melted spread. And here's a tip for lovers of corn-on-the-cob. Instead of slapping butter on a slice of bread and rolling the corn in the bread or the messier process of rolling the corn on the stick of butter (that drove my mother crazy!), spray the corn lightly with the buttery spray while rapidly turning the ear. The coverage imparts all the buttery flavor without all the fat.

There are many products on the market that utilize fat substitutes, drastically reducing the fat content in those foods. You find them in ice cream imitations, salad dressings, cheeses and pastries. These substitutes, however, do not remain stable when subjected to very high temperatures. For this reason you have not yet seen potato chips, French fries or other fried foods available with the fat-free label. Proctor & Gamble has been attempting to acquire approval of Olestra, a new product, from the FDA that will fry like the real thing, reducing a one-ounce serving of potato chips to 67 calories and no fat from the 148 calories and 10 grams of fat in today's regular chip. Other companies, including Arco Chemical Company and Frito-Lay, are in the laboratories trying to successfully present us with an answer to the fat-free fry.

For all you Southerners who can't cook without the flavor of bacon grease, or some kind of salt pork seasoning, there is an answer. There are a number of liquid smoke products available for use in cooking. You must read the list of ingredients before purchase because we found one which included brown sugar and we could not figure out why the beans we prepared were so sweet. The brand we've had the best results from is "Cattlemen's Brand Natural Liquid Smoke," made by French's, the mustard people, in Rochester, New York. Add a touch or two of the liquid smoke to any dish calling for sausage, bacon, ham or salt pork, to taste, and you'll be pleasantly surprised. You'll get the flavor without the meat. Go lightly at first until you become accustomed to using it.

Jim, our dear friend whose name you'll see popping up on the recipe pages, grew up in Arkansas, and knows how to make a mean pot of pinto beans. He was visiting us and very quickly became aware of the manner in which we had become accustomed to eating. He is the kind of guest everyone wants to have. He rolls up his sleeves and pitches in. Your home becomes his home. One day, while David and I were off at work, he fixed a pot of his famous beans, along with rice and corn on the cob. We were greeted by the aroma of country cooking when we returned. The house smelled heavenly. Jim had substituted the liquid smoke for the usual salt pork. This recipe is included for your enjoyment on page 196. And I promise you, you will enjoy it.

Jim experienced more than insight into new ways of preparing old country favorites during his stay. While he kept remarking about how much we eat, and how he'd never eaten so much food, he was shocked at the end of his five week visit. He had lost over seven pounds! That bit of extra padding he'd gradually acquired over the years that had settled around his middle was most definitely disappearing. What a kick! When people are visiting away from home they usually gain weight, not lose it. And he'd had no idea he'd been dropping pounds until he had to move his belt in a notch or two.

The transition in cooking is no more than a simple adjustment of certain ingredients for other ingredients and the exchange of white meat poultry and seafood for beef and other red meats. The use of Molly McButter or Butter Buds, no-stick sprays, lite and fat-free products, skim milk and bouillon or defatted stock, become automatic tradeoffs for the butters and margarines, whole milks and oils. The experimentation and new-found flavors may, in fact, add some excitement to your daily menus. I know that every time we've concocted a new recipe or converted an old one, snipping fat here and cutting fat there, we're so proud of ourselves! Try it!

When computing fat grams for a meal or the entire day's consumption, be honest with yourself. How many people do you know, who, when on a diet, do not include in their daily calorie count the foods they nibble on, while standing in the kitchen. Somehow, standing in the kitchen, tasting while cooking, means they are not eating. What you eat, regardless of your position or placement, matters. However, as we've discussed, the quantity of the RIGHT foods you may consume in this lifestyle is almost limitless. Since these foods are high in fiber you will fill up on these before you overdo in the weight-gain area. Remember the pound of apples at 242 calories as compared to the 250 calories in 1.7 ounces of M&M's?

PORTION-SIZES OF THE RIGHT FOODS

Your only concern when calculating what you eat is food containing fat. And then, your only limit is the amount of grams consumed in a day. Since many of the recipes you'll be preparing are either fat-free or offer only traces of fat, you'll be able to indulge in larger quantities of these foods than you'd have imagined, with no detrimental effect on your weight-loss, or health, for that matter. This is the reason you've seen the claim, repeated numerous times in these pages, that you will not suffer the feelings of denial and deprivation you've experienced before when making changes in your diet.

When dining with others you'll find a "portion" varies according to the person eating that portion. If you've ever paid attention to the plates of food walked away from a buffet table you're familiar with large discrepancies in "serving" sizes. And the little lady with just a scoop of potato salad, three lettuce leaves and four olives smothered in a tablespoon of Roquefort Cheese Dressing has more than ten times the fat grams than the big guy with a plate loaded with fresh veggies, three-bean salad and fruits, with a touch of dressing on the side for fork-dipping.

When reading a recipe it may be difficult to determine the size of a "serving." I've seen some that promise you four servings and, when placed on a plate, a portion would satisfy a five-year-old child, but certainly not an adult. The other day I found a recipe in the *Washington Post* that included all of the nutrients, calories and fat grams per serving for soup to serve four people, yet there was no portion size or total quantity listed to facilitate calculating the values in a one-cup serving. And how do you determine the amount of servings in a bowl of cole slaw or a pot of serve-yourself chili?

We are therefore no longer thinking in terms of "servings." We are, instead, thinking fat grams and satisfaction! For this reason you will find no suggested number of servings listed after the recipes which follow in this book. You may decide that a large bowl of Alaskan Three Bean soup will serve as a filling dinner with a hunk, or two, of sourdough bread. You then may go back to the pot for seconds. Let's not be concerned about the recommended "serving" size. You will find the total quantity you may expect from each of the recipes following the ingredients and directions, along with the total number of fat grams in that recipe. You will then determine the quantity you are consuming, whether it be a cup or one-half the total recipe. The Alaskan Three Bean Soup will yield approximately three quarts, or 12 cups, of soup, depending on how long it cooks and the subsequent water evaporation. The fat grams in the soup total 15, therefore one bowl (16 oz.), or one-sixth of the total recipe, will add 2 1/2 grams of fat to your daily intake. If you indulged in an extra cup of soup as your second helping you totaled less than 4 fat grams for dinner since your bread was, of course, fat-free. You now know how much room you have left in your daily quota for dessert.

You may decide that you want to have the Pasta with Spinach as a side dish with broiled salmon rather than a dinner-sized portion with salad. Although each represents a "serving," you determine what that serving is! One of my favorite dinners is The Vegetable Stir Fry, Thai Shrimp with Basil, and Vegetable Lo Mein, all prepared utilizing the full recipe. We take small portions of each, on steamed rice, as though it were a tasting, rather than a dinner, and have another wonderful dinner to look forward to when we reheat the leftovers! This is a great dinner for guests, too. Don't forget the chopsticks!

You will find some of the recipes in the following section have totals of fat grams in the low to zero range adding only traces to your daily count. These will probably be among your favorites, especially in the early days of your gram-counting. Just be honest with yourself when you're doing your computing. If you eat two chicken breasts, give yourself the extra count. If you don't have the butcher grind the skinned turkey breast for you, don't forget that additional fat you have in the recipe from the prepared ground turkey meat that included skin and fat. You fool no one but yourself if you try to fudge.

Feel free to personalize these and any other recipes you find that fit the low or no-fat requirements. And don't be timid about fat-adjusting some of the old family favorites. Remember that this is not a six-week diet during which time you measure each mouthful and you forget all about it in the seventh week. You'll quickly become accustomed to figuring the fat grams in a complete recipe, and the cumulative amount for the day, without the use of a calculator. In fact, you'll have no need to count after a while. The taste of fatty foods will become less desirable the longer you eat this way and after a while you won't need to count grams to know you are within your limit. You will automatically eat smaller portions of those foods. And you'll always have the labels to guide you. The grams in the foods you're familiar with will become as much a part of you as knowing the way to the supermarket without a map. You'll know just what you've consumed today and will automatically choose the right dinner to round out your day. Or, should I say, slim out your day!

CHAPTER VIII

IN THE BEGINNING

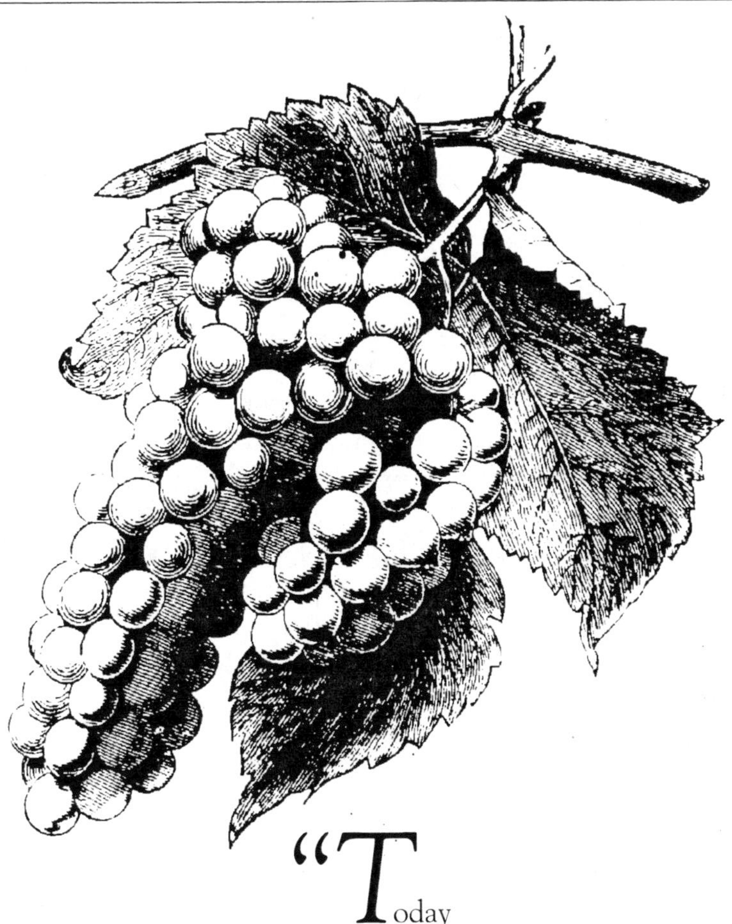

"Today is the first day of the rest of your life!"

This quotation comes to mind whenever starting a new job, moving to a new city or entering a new phase in life. It's always more comfortable when some preparation has been made to accomplish the transition from the old to the new. And here we are. A new lifestyle is about to begin. This is a time of change which you approach with excited anticipation or intrinsic dread.

Relax!

Let's make this transition as simple for you as the trip to the supermarket. And that's where we'll start.

One of the questions most frequently asked by people who are making the initial switch to the fat gram count from the calorie count is, "What should I have on hand to begin?" The answer varies only in the types of food you are already accustomed to including in your diet. If you already enjoy loads of fruits and veggies but you've been preparing them with butter and oils, slight changes in preparation is all that's called for. If you're a meat eater, a switch to chicken breasts, turkey breasts and seafood will be necessary. And if beans and rice have not been a part of your menus, a new love affair is about to begin.

You will find the easiest way to plan your first shopping list is to make a quick visit to your pantry and another to your refrigerator. Once the firm decision to make the change has been made, dump your butter, whole-egg mayonnaise and roquefort cheese dressing. Check the cans, bottles and jars in the pantry and if the oils are second or third on the list of ingredients, do yourself a favor. Deliver these cans to the local homeless shelter where they will do someone else some good. Now you've got some room on the shelves to refill with the kinds of foodstuffs you want to eat from now on.

Check the recipes on the following pages and see which are most appealing to you. Put the necessary items to prepare those recipes on your shopping list. Many of these are already staples in your kitchen. If you want to make the basic foods readily available in addition to the special items for particular recipes, the list which follows will get you going.

Your refrigerator:

Fresh fruits and vegetables. You want to have available to you a mix of these edibles that are hardy and will stay crunchy and flavorful if left in the fridge for a few days. Any delicacies that are short-lived will be an impulse purchase and are not included on this list. Apples and oranges, prunes and raisins will last two weeks or more with no change in the fruit. These are good to have on hand for a nibble or to include with breakfast. Onions, cabbage, green peppers, carrots, and celery are a basis of many of the recipes and are great salad components, as well. The peppers are more perishable than the others listed and will last no more than about a week. The celery lasts longer (up to two to three weeks) in a plastic bag when stored in the vegetable crisper. The carrots, onions and cabbage will stay fresh for even longer than the celery. If they are in your fridge for a longer period of time than a couple of weeks you're buying too large a quantity or you're not eating enough of them!

Replace that mayonnaise with Kraft Free, Smart Beat or Miracle Whip Free. Store some of the tasty fat-free or low-fat salad dressings that taste as good as the real thing such as Kraft Free Peppercorn Ranch or Hidden Valley Low Fat Italian Parmesan (0 grams) or Hidden Valley Ranch Low Fat Honey Dijon Ranch (0 grams per tablespoon). Check the recipes for dressings that look good to you like the Sour Cream Dressing with 0 fat grams on page 144 and pick up the appropriate ingredients.

You may find a new interest in stocking up on some refrigerator staples such as pickles, pickled jalapeños, pepperoncini or pickled beets, hearts of palm and artichoke hearts (packed in water), and other bottled condiments for salad enhancement.

Dairy products such as milk, cream cheese, cottage cheese, yogurt and sour cream should be supplanted by fat-free versions. 2% milk sounds great but most people who think that means 2 grams of fat per 8-ounce glass would be shocked to find out there are 5 grams of fat in 2% milk, 2 1/2 grams of fat in 1% milk. Go for skimmed milk and within 3 to 4 weeks you'll wonder why you resisted the fat-free stuff. You'll grow accustomed to the difference. There is no contest on the replacement for the full-fat cream cheese. Philadelphia Free, with no grams, tastes just like the stuff they make with 10 grams per ounce. There is no longer a need for sweet cream butter and eventually you will not have a need for margarine (even the low-fat variety). Keep a package or two of fat-free cheese slices available for sandwiches (Borden Lite Line gets our vote for flavor), and Healthy Choice Fat Free Nonfat Pasteurized Cheese Product for baking in potatoes and casseroles.

It doesn't take much room to store a can or two of water-packed tuna in the fridge so it's chilled for salads or a quick sandwich. And do keep a jar of preserves to go with that bagel and fat-free cream cheese. The variance of fullness of flavor in different preserves or fruit spreads is remarkable. Try the Polaner All Fruit Black Cherry. What a treat!

And don't forget to pick up some Entenmann's Fat-Free or SnackWell's goodies if you have a sweet tooth because you don't want to be caught with a raging attack and go for the other kind of sweet snack. Check out Archway Fat Free Oatmeal Raisin Cookies. They are chewy and satisfying. And there are Fat Free Newtons in a variety of fruits from fig to apple with the flavor of the original. As with so many of these goodies...let your taster be your guide. I've listed these with refrigerator items because some of these products stay fresher when refrigerated.

Your freezer:

Fat-free breads, bagels and pita will need only a turn in the oven to taste fresh when stored in the freezer in freezer-proof plastic bags. Beans, pastas and rice, prepared in volume and stored in freezer bags are ready at a moment's notice, when you're ready. The pasta is thawed by placing in a colander or strainer under hot running water. The rice and beans can be thawed, quickly, in the microwave: on high, partially covered, for 3 minutes, stir, check for doneness and repeat until done.

Keep leftovers, or meal-size packages of foods that you've prepared on weekends, ready for thawing, reheating and serving for weekday dinners. Pyrex has rectangular storage bowls in assorted sizes with plastic tops, that store in very little space, stack for optimum usage in the freezer, and can go from the freezer to the microwave or oven (without the cover, of course), to the refrigerator or dishwasher. A boon for the busy kitchen and a time-saver for you.

You will find a host of wonderful frozen vegetables that can be thawed by simply running under cold water for use in salads, stir-fry and stews or soups. You can buy most of them in giant economy-sized bags, remove the amount you need, and store the balance in the same bag, using a twistie.

Remember when stocking (or should I say, re-stocking) your freezer, the only kind of frozen desserts that find their way in there are fat-free or a make-believe ice cream that is truly low-fat. There are some ice milks out there with 5 grams of fat per 1/2 cup. If you're a real ice cream lover a 1/2 cup serving is a teaser and before you know it, you've devoured a cup and a half. Healthy Choice, one of the best tasting, "real-ice-cream-like" desserts we've found is 2 grams per 1/2 cup. And if you're going to go crazy, better to do it with 6 grams instead of 15! Depending on what you had earlier in the day, you're probably within your 20 grams and that ice cream is so good to look forward to!

Your pantry:

Here we can go on all day but we're talking about a minimum start-up until you know exactly which dishes are your favorites. You want to be sure that any and all dried spices that you've enjoyed in the past remain fresh and don't lose their place of honor. If you don't have a container of dried mixed Italian herbs, you will probably want to stock one. Check your recipes and see which additional herbs you may want to stock for seasoning. The granulated bouillon, soy sauce, garlic and, if you will use dry white wine for sautéing, the wine should be included, in preparation for cooking. Buy a Dry Sherry or Chablis rather than any of the bottled "cooking wines" which are extremely salty and are overpriced, as well.

Stock regular Pam, Mazola Spray or Wesson Oil Spray and Weight Watchers Buttery Spray, Olive Oil Pam, Molly McButter and Butter Buds.

You'll find that an assortment of low-fat soups, to which you may add rice and/or beans (canned or cooked), will come in handy on evenings when the shoes come off on the way in the door and the thought of anything other than opening a can is horrifying. The cooked rice is in a plastic bag in the freezer waiting for this occasion. By the way, Health Valley makes a wonderful canned Fat-Free Chili with Black Beans for use on nights like this.

Brown or white rice is a must. Uncle Ben's and assorted other brands cook differently with different measures of water, some cold and some boiling, so read the directions and take nothing for granted. Different recipes sometimes specify one rice over another and it is important to get that right or the dish can turn out wrong. Tammy, the sweetest, prettiest oral hygienist I've ever known, has always used Minute Rice. With two babies, one and two years old, and a full-time job, you can understand her need for quick and easy cooking. She fixed one of my recipes and told me later that, having used Minute Rice instead of Uncle Ben's Converted Rice, she ended up with a bowl of glop instead of individual grains of edible rice.

Beans, both dry and canned, should be readily available in your pantry for all kinds of meals. The dry, which is a heck of a money-saver, for those days you have time to cook (the directions for fool-proof beans is on page 193), and the canned for those days you don't. Be sure to cut down on the salt in the recipes when using canned beans because those beans have salt already added. Remember to use beans...with rice, in canned soups and salads. They are extra nourishing and add the fiber that will fill your tummy and keep your system humming, too.

Stick a few potatoes, white and sweet, redskin and Idaho, in the pantry, too, for baking as a starch with dinner, for making potato salad, or as a meal with Molly McButter, fat-free sour cream, Bacos and some vegetables to round out the meal. Pasta for all the neat pasta dishes you will prepare should be the eggless variety and you will want to have some canned plum tomatoes to make sweet, tomato-based sauces. If you're going to try some of the Oriental dishes, place a bag of Shitake mushrooms and some Oyster Sauce, some Szechuan Sauce, low-sodium soy sauce, and perhaps a jar of Chili Puree with Garlic Sauce in the pantry, too.

This should get you started, and you'll probably add a bunch to the list from my recipes that follow, or others you are anxious to try, that are low-fat or can be prepared so that they are low-fat.

The biggest surprise for you is yet to come, when you start this lifestyle and discover the wonderful flavors and delicious foods you've yet to enjoy...all in the name of good health and good looks!

BON APPETIT!!

CHAPTER IX

RECIPES & GOODIES

You've had an opportunity to explore a different approach to satisfying the need for a more healthful lifestyle and a more enlightened relationship with the foods you love.

In the following pages you will find over 250 recipes that have been designed to excite your tast buds and fulfill your need for hearty, satisfying, "feel good" foods, all presented to you with the goal of helping you to love living low fat.

HORS D'OEUVRES

Most hors d'oeuvre spreads and dips require a cracker, toasted bread point or chip. A great many of the crackers available are high in fat grams, including a number of the popular brands...8 Wheat Thins, 3 grams; 4 Pepperidge Farms Hearty Wheat, 4 grams; 4 Ritz, 4 grams; 5 Keebler Toasted Rye, 4 grams; 3 Triscuits, 2 grams. The "low-fat" varieties are not necessarily what we consider sufficiently low in fat for our way of eating so check the reduced gram count for the same amount of crackers. Keep your eye on the labels of any brands you decide to use.

Just as there are the high-fat choices, there are, also, some great low-fat alternatives. Listed here, for your convenience, are a variety of such crunchy doodads.

Melba Toast (rye, white or pumpernickel)	**5 pieces**	**0 fat grams**
Fat Free Pita (cut into triangles and toasted)	**2 pockets**	**0 fat grams**
Rice Cakes	**5 pieces**	**0 fat grams**
Ak-Mak Original (Sesame Cracker)	**1 cracker**	**less than 1 gram**
Kavil Norwegian	**3–4 pieces**	**less than 1 gram**
Saltines	**5 pieces**	**1 fat gram**
Wasa Extra Crisp Cracker-bread	**1 piece**	**less than 1 gram**
Wasa Golden Rye Crisp bread	**1 piece**	**0 fat grams**
Fat-Free Corn Tortilla	**1 piece**	**0 fat grams**
Fat-Free Flour Tortilla	**1 piece**	**0 fat grams**
Fat Free White, Whole Wheat, or Pumpernickel Bread, toasted (cut in rounds or triangles)	**1 piece**	**0 fat grams**
Pretzels (most varieties)	**1 ounce**	**1 fat gram**
Crispy Fresh Vegetables in slices or sticks	**1 piece**	**0 fat grams**
Mr. Phipps Fat Free Pretzel crackers	**6 pieces**	**0 fat grams**

CAPONATA

This Italian appetizer is an old favorite and retains the flavor of the original. Serve this with toasted bread or pita triangles.

1 medium eggplant (about 1-1/2 pounds), diced
1 medium onion, chopped
1 stalk celery, chopped
2 cloves garlic, minced
1 green bell pepper, chopped
Olive Oil Pam
3/4 cup defatted chicken stock
4 oz. pimento-stuffed green olives, sliced
3 oz. bottled capers with liquid
1 Tbs. sugar
3 oz. (1/2 small can) tomato paste
Salt and pepper to taste

Soak the diced eggplant in salted water about 30 minutes. Drain the water. Sauté the onion, celery, garlic and bell pepper in Olive Oil Pam until soft. Add a bit of the stock to the mixture if too dry. When the vegetables are soft, add the tomato paste and cook well. Add water, sugar, salt and pepper and cook until thick. Add olives, capers and eggplant. Simmer 10 minutes. Remove from heat, allow to cool to room temperature and serve. If prepared ahead of time, refrigerate until about 1/2 hour before serving. Serve at room temperature.

Yield: 3—4 cups
Total Fat Grams: 8

HERB-STUFFED MUSHROOMS

Be sure to choose firm, large mushrooms for this old favorite so that they won't fall apart when you stuff them.

12 large fresh mushrooms
1/2 cup white wine
2 tsp. beef bouillon granules
1/4 cup finely chopped onion
2 packets Butter Buds, made into liquid
1/2 cup packaged herb-seasoned stuffing mix

Wash mushrooms, remove the stems and set the stems aside. In medium-sized saucepan heat the wine and bouillon. Add the mushroom caps, tops down, and simmer, covered, for 2 to 3 minutes. Remove the mushrooms and set aside. Reserve the wine mixture. Chop the mushroom stems and combine with onion, 1/2 cup Butter Buds and 1/4 cup wine mixture. Place in separate saucepan and cook over medium heat until vegetables are tender, about 2 to 3 minutes. Stir in the stuffing. Place about a tablespoon of stuffing in each mushroom cap. Brush with Butter Buds liquid and place under broiler for about 2 to 3 minutes until hot.

Yield: 12 Stuffed Caps
Total Fat Grams: Traces

CRAB CURRY SPREAD

Try a little more curry in this mixture if you prefer a heavier flavor.

1 cup crabmeat, flaked or lump
2 Tbs. fresh parsley, snipped
1 Tbs. onion, minced
3 Tbs. fat-free mayonnaise
1 dash Dijon mustard
1/4 tsp. curry powder
1 tsp. fresh lemon juice

Flake or dice the crabmeat. Add all ingredients to the crab and toss until well mixed. Refrigerate and serve with crackers, toasted fat-free bread rounds or melba toast.

Yield: 1 cup
Total Fat Grams: 5

MINI CRABCAKES

2 cans crabmeat (6 Oz. each), rinsed and drained
2 egg whites, lightly beaten
1 1/4 cups fat-free sour cream, divided
1 cup chopped green onions, divided
1 Tbs. fresh lemon juice
1 cup fresh fat-free whole wheat breadcrumbs
1 tsp. dried dill
1 lemon, cut in wedges

In a large bowl blend the crab, egg whites, 1/4 cup sour cream 1/2 cup green onions and lemon juice. Form Mixture into 1-inch patties. Combine breadcrumbs and dill. Roll the cakes in the crumb mixture. Place on large nonstick baking sheet and bake for 10 to 15 minutes at 375°. Garnish with the lemon wedges and with the sour cream-green onion mixture for sauce.

Yield: 16—20 cakes
Total Fat Grams: 12

SALMON CAPER SPREAD

1 can (15 1/2 oz.) pink Alaskan salmon, drained
1 Tbs. prepared horseradish
2 tsp. bottled capers
2 Tbs. fat-free mayonnaise
2 tsp. fresh lemon juice

Remove any bones or skin from the salmon. Mix together all ingredients. Add more mayonnaise if necessary for a smooth spread.

Prepare ahead of time and refrigerate until serving, if desired. Serve with crackers or toasted bread squares.

Yield: 1 1/2 cups
Total Fat Grams: 18

SALMON PÂTÉ TRIANGLES

This hors d'oeuvre is a variation of the Salmon Caper Spread. Dill is a natural enhancement for the flavor of salmon and the two are often combined. Both recipes, this and the Salmon Caper Spread, are higher in fat than many of the other hors d'oeuvres because of the high fat content of the salmon, so eat sparingly.

1 can (15 1/2 oz.) pink Alaskan salmon, drained
1 Tbs. fat-free mayonnaise
1 tsp. dried dill
1/2 tsp. freshly ground black pepper
2 tsp. fresh lemon juice

Remove any bone or skin from the salmon. Mix together all ingredients. Add more mayonnaise if necessary for a smooth spread. This spread can be made ahead of time and refrigerated until serving. Serve cold or at room temperature on toasted fat-free bread cut into triangles.

Yield: 1 1/2 cup
Total Fat Grams: 18

BOILED SHRIMP

An old favorite, this hors d'oeuvre is one of this country's most popular appetizers. The crushed red pepper will give the shrimp a little extra lift.

1 pound shrimp, cleaned and deveined
1 Tbs. whole peppercorns
1 tsp. dried oregano
1 Tbs. dried parsley, or a bunch of fresh parsley
2 ribs fresh celery including the tops
1 tsp. dried, crushed, hot red pepper
1 small onion, quartered

Remove shells, clean and devein the shrimp. Place in 1 quart cold water in medium-sized pot with all other ingredients. Bring to a boil. When shrimp turn pink and start to curl, drain in a strainer or colander. Run under cold water, removing any seasoning particles which may cling. Refrigerate until well-chilled. Serve with Spicy Red Cocktail Sauce (page 147) or Remoulade Sauce (page 146).

Yield: 1 pound shrimp
Total Fat Grams: 4

PIQUANT SHRIMP ROUNDS

Everyone loves shrimp and this appetizer is a zippy version of an old favorite. Add a bit of Louisiana hot sauce if you like more spice.

3 Tbs. fat-free mayonnaise
2 tsp. pickle relish
3 Tbs. chili sauce
1/2 tsp. prepared horseradish
1/4 tsp. fresh lemon juice
4 slices fat-free bread
8 boiled shrimp

Mix together all ingredients except shrimp and bread. Use a biscuit cutter or small glass to cut 4 rounds from each slice of bread. Slice each shrimp, lengthwise, into two halves. Spread the top of each round of bread with the mixture and top with the half-shrimp.
Serve at once.

Yield: 16 rounds
Total fat grams: 2

GARLIC SHRIMP

Now here's an hor d'oeuvre that will surprise you. So simple and so good. If you are out of fresh garlic (heaven forbid!) sprinkle garlic powder on the shrimp as it's sautéing. This dish can be added atop pasta with Marinara Sauce. Place a couple of sprigs of fresh parsley and basil here and there and you've got a dish for a cookbook cover.

1 pound shrimp, cleaned and deveined
1 tsp. garlic, minced
Olive Oil Pam
1/4 cup dry white wine

Clean and devein the shrimp. Spray the Pam on the surface of a non-stick pan. Cook the shrimp and garlic on a high heat, stirring briskly. Do not scorch the garlic. As soon as the shrimp start turning pink, add the wine and cook about 1 minute, or until the shrimp curl.
Serve at room temperature.

Yield: 1 pound shrimp
Total Fat Grams: 9

GRILLED SHRIMP

When you look at this recipe, don't let the options confuse you. Broiled outdoors the flavor is superb, as is. Indoors, you may want to use a few seasonings to enhance the flavor. Either way, these hors d'oeuvres are succulent.

1 pound jumbo or large shrimp, cleaned and deveined
Buttery or Olive Oil Spray, optional
Liquid smoke, optional
Garlic or onion powder, optional

Peel and clean the shrimp. Place on aluminum foil and spray with Olive Oil Pam or Weight Watchers Buttery Spray, or as another option, brush with liquid smoke, and place on grill outdoors or in the oven under the broiler. If grilled outdoors, no flavoring is necessary because the taste of the charcoal is so good. You might want to roll the shrimp in garlic powder or onion powder before grilling indoors for added flavor.
Serve with fresh lemon wedges.

Yield: 1 pound shrimp
Total Fat Grams: 8 to 10

SHRIMP SPREAD

Let's talk about easy! If you have these ingredients in your home all the time, you'll never be caught without something to serve…and fast!

1 can baby shrimp
1 Tbs. fat-free mayonnaise
Dash hot pepper sauce
1 tsp. fresh lemon juice

Remove shrimp from can, run under cold water and refrigerate for about 20 minutes. Mix all ingredients. Season with hot pepper sauce and lemon juice to taste.
Serve with Melba Rounds.

Yield: 3/4 cup
Total Fat Grams: 3

SPICY HOT ORIENTAL SHRIMP

The Oriental Chili Sauce with Garlic is available in a small jar. You'll find it in Oriental food markets and sometimes in the foreign food section of your grocery store. You will see additional recipes in this book calling for this condiment. This is definitely spicy.

1 Tbs. dry white wine or chicken broth
3 Tbs. shallots, minced
1 1/2 pounds large shrimp, peeled and deveined
1 Tbs. Oriental Chili Sauce with Garlic
3 Tbs. fresh lemon juice
Salt and freshly ground pepper to taste

Heat wine or broth and add shallots. Cook 1 minute and add shrimp, cooking for 1 minute or until pink. Place shrimp in medium bowl with Chili Sauce with Garlic and lemon juice. Season with salt and pepper.
Refrigerate for 2 to 3 hours. Drain shrimp and serve.

Yield: 1 1/2 pounds shrimp
Total Fat Grams: 12

TUNA CURRY ROLL-UPS

Make sure your bread is very fresh so that you can roll the slice around the tuna mixture without the bread cracking or splitting.

1 can (6 1/2 oz.) waterpack tuna fish
1/2 cup fat-free mayonnaise, plus 2 Tbs.
1/2 tsp. onion salt
1/2 tsp. curry powder
14 slices fat-free whole wheat bread
Paprika

Trim crusts from bread slices. The crusts can be cut into cubes and toasted for use as croutons for salad or soup. Drain the tuna. Combine tuna, mayonnaise (except the additional 2 Tbs.), onion salt, and curry powder. Use the 2 Tbs. mayonnaise to spread on the bread slices. Place a small amount of the tuna mixture on each slice of bread and roll up. If necessary use a toothpick to hold the bread roll in place. Refrigerate for 24 hours.
Remove from the refrigerator and slice into 1/4 inch to 1/2 inch slices. Place on a baking tray, sprinkle with paprika and broil until the bread is lightly toasted.
Serve warm.

Yield: 70 to 85 rounds
Total Fat Grams: 4

TUNA CURRY ROLL-UP MELTS

Follow the same recipe as the TUNA CURRY ROLL-UPS. After broiling the rollups until the bread is lightly toasted, place a chip of Healthy Choice Pasteurized Process Cheese Product, or Fat Free Grated Cheddar, on each roll-up and return to the broiler until the cheese melts. Serve immediately. The yield and fat grams remain the same since the cheese is fat free.

TUNA SPREAD

2 cans (6 1/2 oz.) waterpack tuna fish
1 Tbs. fat-free mayonnaise
1 tsp. parsley, freshly chopped
1/2 tsp. onion, minced fine, optional
1 tsp. fresh lemon
Cherry tomatoes for garnish

Mix all ingredients, mashing tuna with a fork. Add more mayonnaise, if necessary, for a smooth spread. Place mixture on crackers or toasted bread rounds. Slices of cherry tomatoes may be placed on top, when serving.

Yield: 65 to 75
Total Fat Grams: 7

CURRIED CLAM DOLLARS

1 12 ounce container Philadelphia Free
1 can (6 1/2 oz.) chopped clams
1/2 tsp. garlic powder
1 tsp. soy sauce
4 or 5 slices fat-free white bread, cut in rounds
Curry powder

Leave the cream cheese at room temperature for about an hour to soften. Drain the clam juice and gradually add this liquid to the cream cheese, blending and softening the cheese until you have a smooth, spreadable consistency. Discard the rest of the juice. Add the clams, garlic and soy sauce and blend thoroughly. Generously spread on bread rounds, sprinkle with curry powder and bake at 375° until the curry melts and the cream cheese is hot, about 10 to 15 minutes.

Yield: 16 to 20 rounds
Total Fat Grams: 1/2

CUCUMBER TURKEY SPREAD

1 can (12 1/2 oz.) white-meat turkey, chopped
1/2 cup cucumber, finely chopped
2 Tbs. fat-free mayonnaise
1/2 tsp. Tabasco
Salt and pepper, or seasoned pepper, to taste

Combine chopped turkey and mayonnaise. Add remaining ingredients and mix until blended. Serve chilled with crackers.

Yield: 1 1/2 cups
Total Fat Grams: 7

CHICKEN WON TON APPETIZER

You will use a wok in preparing this hors d'oeuvre. While the preparation of this recipe is more time-consuming than most of the others, it is worth the investment. Some of the ingredients which are necessary for Oriental food preparation are included in this dish and I have found them in the foreign food section of my supermarket. However, if your store doesn't stock Oriental products, look for an Oriental food market where you can find these and other exotic products to experiment with. Try to buy fresh bean sprouts for this recipe. The canned variety adds a definite "tinny" taste to the other ingredients.

1 Tbs. cornstarch
3 Tbs. water
1 boneless chicken breast, skinned and minced
1/2 Tbs. defatted chicken stock or broth
1 tsp. ginger root, minced
3/4 cup celery, minced
1/4 cup green onions, minced
1/2 cup bamboo shoots, minced
1/4 pound bean sprouts, rinsed, drained, blotted dry and chopped
1 Tbs. Hoisin sauce
1 1/2 tsp. soy sauce
24 won ton wrappers

Mix the cornstarch in the water until smooth and set aside. Microwave the chicken breast on high for 3 minutes. When the chicken is white in the center, set aside. Heat the stock or broth in the wok and add ginger root, celery and green onions. Stir-fry 1 minute or until veggies are crisp-tender. Stir in bamboo shoots and bean sprouts, then cornstarch mixture, Hoisin sauce, soy sauce and cooked chicken. Set mixture aside.

Remove won ton wrappers from package. Cover with a

damp cloth to prevent them from drying out as you work. Take one wrapper and place it with one corner facing you. Place 1 teaspoon of filling in the center of the wrapper. Moisten the edges of the wrapper with water, fold over to make a triangle and press down the edges to seal. Repeat until all won ton are prepared. Bring water to a simmer in a 2 quart pot. Put about 6 won ton in the water at a time. Poach for 4 to 5 minutes. Remove with a slotted spoon and drain on paper towels. Repeat until all won ton are cooked.

Serve hot or at room temperature with additional soy sauce for dipping.

Yield: 24 won tons or dumplings
Total Fat Grams: 8

BEAN BURRITO CANAPÉS

This is a two-day treat because the burrito needs time to "set up" for slicing on the second day. Jim's Beans (page 196), 1 1/2 cups, can be used instead of the canned beans. Be sure to drain some of the liquid.

1 can Old El Paso Mexe-Beans, partially drained
1/2 medium green bell pepper, minced
1/2 medium onion, chopped
2 oz. Healthy Choice Pasteurized Process Cheese Product
Bottled jalapeño pepper slices, optional
12 fat-free flour tortillas

Cook beans, onion and bell pepper until heated through. Mash the beans leaving some lumps. Cook down until mixture is pasty (if you have little or no preparation time, a can of Old El Paso Fat Free Refried Beans can be used). Spread mixture on flour tortillas and roll. Refrigerate for 24 hours. Remove from refrigerator, slice into 1/2 to 3/4 inch rounds and place on cookie sheet with a small piece of cheese on each round and top with a jalapeño pepper slice. Heat at 400° until cheese melts. Serve at once.

Yield: 50 to 55 rounds
Total Fat Grams: Less than 1

MARINATED MUSHROOMS

Served cold, toothpicks for skewering, makes this a tasty addition to a relish tray. Keep these mushrooms in mind as a salad add-on, as well.

1 jar (5 oz.) button mushrooms
3 Tbs. fat-free French or Italian salad dressing
1 Tbs. freshly snipped parsley or 1 tsp. dried, minced parsley
Dash garlic powder, optional
Dash hot pepper sauce, optional

Toss all ingredients and refrigerate. Serve chilled.

Yield: 1/2 to 3/4 cup
Total Fat Grams: 0

CREAMY SPINACH DIP

When our sister Judy Walz mixed this dip she was short on yogurt and substituted 1 cup fat-free sour cream for that amount of yogurt. It was scrumptious.

1 package (10 oz.) frozen chopped spinach
1/4 package fat-free, dry, vegetable soup mix
1 3/4 cup plain non-fat yogurt
1/4 cup fat-free mayonnaise
1 can (8 Oz.) water chestnuts, drained and chopped
2 Tbs. chopped chives
1/8 tsp. garlic powder

Thaw spinach in the microwave and drain. Squeeze any excess liquid out with your hands. Stir dry soup mix thoroughly before measuring to assure an evenly distributed mixture. Combine all ingredients and mix thoroughly. Chill for at least 2 hours and serve with fresh vegetables such as carrot sticks, cucumber slices, celery sticks and bell pepper strips.

Yield: 4 cups
Total Fat Grams: 0

BARI'S CLAM DIP

There is never a get-together at Bari's that she is not coaxed into preparing this wonderful dip. It's a winner that has practically no fat depending on the crackers or pita you serve.

1 container (8 oz.) fat-free cream cheese
1 can (6 1/2 oz.) chopped clams, drained
3 dashes Worcestershire sauce
1 tsp. granulated vegetable bouillon
1/4 tsp. garlic powder
3 dashes Tabasco

Mix all ingredients and chill. Serve with crackers or pita chips.

Yield: 2 cups
Total Fat Grams: 1

CHILI CON QUESO
(Mexican Cheese Dip)

This is the most popular dip ever served. It's been around for years and people never get tired of it. In fact, you can use some of this dip, added when the eggs start to set when your scrambling your Egg Beaters for breakfast or brunch, to add additional flavor and color; with The Bean Dip that follows for rolling in tortillas; on chips to make Nachos (page 114); and dribble some in salads to turn an American salad into a Taco Salad (page 134). You'll find a bunch of exciting uses for this dip yourself as you dress up everyday foods. The leftover dip stores well in the refrigerator and should be reheated in the microwave for more thorough enjoyment!

1/2 onion, minced fine
1/2 green bell pepper, minced fine
1 package Healthy Choice Pasteurized Process Cheese Product (2 lb.), broken up into about 8 to 10 pieces
2 cans Rotel Diced Tomatoes and Green Chilies, reserve juice
Pickled jalapeño peppers, sliced, to taste (optional)

Combine all ingredients except the juice from the Rotel and the jalapeño pepper slices. Place in a microwave-proof bowl, loosely covered, and cook on high for 5 minutes. Mix and return to microwave for additional 5 minute intervals until the cheese is thoroughly melted. If too thick, add some of the reserved juice and reheat for 2 minutes. The jalapeños may be added, sparingly, if a hotter version is desired, or may be served on the side for individual taste adjustment.

Yield: About 5 to 6 cups
Total Fat Grams: 0

BEAN DIP

1 can (15 Oz.) Old El Paso Mexe-Beans, drained
1 medium onion, chopped fine
1 small green bell pepper, minced
Dash garlic powder
1 tsp. salsa (thick and chunky)

Cook the beans in a medium-sized saucepan with the onion, green bell pepper and garlic, until the onions and peppers are soft. Mash well or blend in a food processor. Add salsa and mix thoroughly. Serve at room temperature with baked corn tortillas cut in triangles or pita triangles with Salsa (page 149) on the side. Freeze any leftover dip after 3 days.

Yield: 1 1/2 cup
Total Fat Grams: Less than 1

BEAN AND CHEESE NACHOS

Here's a chance to make a wonderful nibble or appetizer that looks extravagant and may just be leftovers from last week's party that you've pulled together. If the Bean Dip has been frozen, a quick turn in the microwave will thaw it out and you're ready. If you haven't got the Chili Con Queso already prepared, the grated cheddar will do nicely.

5 fat-free corn tortillas, cut in 8 wedges each
1 cup Bean Dip (page 113)
1 cup Chili Con Queso (page 112) or non-fat grated cheddar cheese
Pickled jalapeño peppers, sliced

Separate the wedges on a cookie sheet. Bake at 375° until dry and crisp. Do not burn them. Check them after 5 minutes and if they are dry on top but moist underneath, flip them over. When they are ready, let them cool for about 5 minutes. These can be made ahead of time and stored in an airtight container.

Cover the chips evenly with the Bean Dip. Repeat process with the Chili Con Queso, or sprinkle with grated cheddar cheese. Replace in oven until cheese melts, about 3 to 4 minutes. If you like them hot you may place a jalapeño pepper slice on each of the 40 nachos, or serve them on the side for your braver friends. Serve with Salsa (page 149) on the side.

Yield: 40 nachos
Total Fat Grams: 2

SUPER-DUPER NACHOS

This is a variation of the preceding recipe. The addition of the salad stuff makes a more impressive presentation and lightens up the taste. See which way you like it better.

5 fat-free corn tortillas, cut in 8 wedges each
1 cup Bean Dip
1 cup Chili Con Queso, or grated cheddar cheese
1 cup lettuce, chopped or sliced thin
3/4 cup tomatoes, chopped
Pickled jalapeño peppers, sliced

Prepare as above in recipe for Bean and Cheese Nachos. After removing from the oven sprinkle with the lettuce and tomato, add the pepper slices to taste. Serve immediately.

Yield: 40 Nachos
Total Fat Grams: 2

FRENCH ONION DIP

Enjoy the famous California Dip with a slight adjustment to make it a low-fat delight. Really a satisfier served with fresh veggies or Mr. Phipps Fat Free Pretzel Chips.

1 pint fat-free sour cream
1 package Lipton's Onion Soup Mix

Combine ingredients. Refrigerate. Serve chilled.

Yield: 2 cups
Total Fat Grams: 1

ANTIPASTO

This Italian masterpiece can be served as an hors d'oeuvre or a salad to lend an exciting start to almost any meal. The number of vegetables you choose to include on the platter, and the amount of each, is a decision which can be made based on the veggies you have on hand or you want to use for variety of color and taste. In other words, do your thing! You'll find the quantities listed below, if all vegetables are included, will serve a group of approximately twenty people as a nibbler along with other hors d'oeuvres. As a salad or meal starter it will feed only half as many.

2 cups carrot sticks
2 cups celery sticks
2 medium green bell peppers, sliced
2 medium red bell peppers, sliced
1 cup mushroom caps
1 cup cherry tomatoes
1 cup broccoli flowerets
1 cup cauliflower pieces
1/2 pound steamed, fresh asparagus
1 cup cucumber slices, skin on for color
1 jar roasted peppers, drained
1/2 cup bottled pickled beets
1/2 cup bottled pickled okra
1 cup Marinated Mixed Beans (page 123)
1 cup artichoke hearts, packed in water, drained
1/2 cup hearts of palm
1/2 cup sliced radishes
Romaine lettuce leaves
Our Creamy Italian Dressing (page 142)

Clean and prepare all the vegetables and set aside. Clean the lettuce leaves and spin-dry or pat dry with paper towels. Layer the lettuce leaves on a large platter and arrange the vegetables on the leaves. Serve chilled with the dressing on the side for dipping or dribbling.

Total Fat Grams: Varies between traces and 1, for beans

SALADS & SALAD DRESSINGS

The salad has always been considered the dieter's answer to the weight loss question and the solution to maintaining a trim, slim figure. How often have you heard the statement, "Let's go for a light lunch today. There's that salad bar down the street that has 55 items!"

It's true that all those colorful veggies, crispy, crunchy and bursting with flavor, are just the thing for curbing the appetite and whittling the waist. And since a number of vegetables such as broccoli and carrots are loaded with the cancer-fighter, beta-carotene, these vegetables are that much more attractive to the health-minded populace. As the precursor to a delightful dinner, or as the entree, itself, the salad can be splendid.

There are so many salads and dressings that are delicious and low-fat, and offer a variety of flavors and textures, a plus in the satisfaction quotient. Spend some time trying different fat-free dressings that you'll find on your grocer's shelves, too. The array of these dressings has expanded as the low-fat lifestyle has become more and more accepted in our society.

You will find, in this section of the book, a number of salads you'll recognize like cole slaw and potato salad, some exotic salads such as Chinese Asparagus Salad and Red Sunset Salad, and an assortment of dressings that will help keep you in shape.

If you're preparing the salad at home, one tool you will find helpful is a salad spinner. The advantage of the spin-dry for your lettuce leaves is the speed with which the spinner removes the water clinging to the leaves while no bruising occurs. The full flavor of the dressing, then, is not diluted by the droplets that well may adhere to the lettuce or spinach if not properly dried, and the spinner eliminates the problem of wilting.

FRUIT SALAD

This is a refreshing appetizer that may be a meal with the addition of fat-free cottage cheese, sorbet or fat-free sherbet. Use your imagination on this one and use any fruits that appeal to you to add color and flavor. The only fruit that may be considered taboo is coconut because of the fat content.

2 oranges, peeled and cubed
2 apples, cubed
1 banana, cubed
1 bunch seedless grapes
1 can assorted fruit chunks in natural juices
1 grapefruit, meat only, in sections
1 cup frozen orange juice concentrate, undiluted

Combine all ingredients and any additional fruits of your choice such as peaches, peeled and cubed, plums, prunes, dates or raisins. Refrigerate. Serve chilled.

Yield: Varies according to your additions.
Total Fat Grams: 1

CARROT AND RAISIN SALAD

You've enjoyed this salad at a number of salad bars, now here's the low-fat version for you to pack with lunch, to take the place of cole slaw with your sandwich.

2 cups grated carrot
1/2 cup raisins
1/4 cup pineapple chunks
1/2 cup fat-free mayonnaise
3/4 tsp. salt
1/2 tsp. sugar, optional
1 Tbs. fresh lemon juice or vinegar
Freshly ground black pepper to taste

Place carrots, raisins and pineapple in a bowl and set aside. Mix together the mayonnaise, salt, sugar, lemon juice and pepper. Add this mayo mixture to the carrot mixture and toss to combine thoroughly. Refrigerate for at least 4 hours for flavors to blend, before serving.

Yield: 3 cups
Total Fat Grams: Traces

MARINATED MIXED BEANS

1 can green beans or 1 box frozen green beans, thawed in the microwave for 1 minute
1 can wax beans
1 can garbanzo beans, rinsed and drained
1 can red beans, drained
1 large onion, sliced very thin (Vidalia, if available)
4 to 6 Tbs. fat-free Italian salad dressing

Combine all ingredients. Refrigerate for at least 24 hours before serving.

Yield: 7 to 8 cups
Total Fat Grams: 2

REDSKIN POTATO SALAD

You'll be amazed at how good this potato salad tastes. They'll never guess!

1 1/2 pounds small redskin potatoes
4 ribs celery, minced
1/4 medium onion, minced
1/2 red bell pepper, minced
3/4 cup fat-free mayonnaise
1/4 cup vinegar
1 1/2 Tbs. Dijon mustard
3/4 tsp. salt
Seasoned Pepper to taste

Scrub the potatoes and cut into cubes, with the skins on. Place in cold, salted water and bring to a boil. Cook for about 10 to 15 minutes or until the potatoes are firm but can be pierced with a fork. Do not cook until they are soft! Set aside and let cool to room temperature. Mince celery, onion and bell pepper and set aside. Mix together mayo, vinegar, mustard and salt. Combine all ingredients including the potatoes, toss well and add seasoned pepper to taste. Refrigerate for at least 4 hours for flavors to blend. Serve chilled.

Yield: 5 to 6 cups
Total Fat Grams: 1

COLE SLAW

This old favorite can now be enjoyed without worrying about quantities consumed. The cabbage collapses as it stands in the dressing so your yield will not be as great in volume as when the ingredients are initially mixed.

4 cups shredded cabbage
1 cup grated carrots
1/2 medium green bell pepper, minced
1/2 cup fat-free mayonnaise
1/8 tsp. Dijon mustard
1/2 tsp. sugar
1 Tbs. vinegar
1 Tbs. skim milk
3/4 tsp. salt
Freshly ground black pepper to taste

Place cabbage, carrot and bell pepper in a large bowl. Set aside. Combine the mayo, mustard, sugar and vinegar. Stir well. Mix in the milk, salt and pepper, and add to the cabbage and other vegetables. Toss well and refrigerate for at least 4 hours before serving.

Yield: 5 to 6 cups
Total Fat Grams: Less than 1

COLE SLAW, TOO

This slaw is an adapted version of the original recipe which has a bit more zip because of the Italian seasonings in the Good Seasonings salad dressing mix. It is just as easy to prepare as the original.

4 cups shredded cabbage
1 cup grated carrots
1/2 medium green bell pepper, minced
1/2 cup to 3/4 cup Our Creamy Italian Dressing (page 142)
1/2 tsp. sugar
1 Tbs. vinegar
Freshly ground black pepper to taste

Place the cabbage, carrot and bell pepper in a large bowl. Set aside. Combine remaining ingredients and add to cabbage and vegetables. Toss well and refrigerate for at least 4 hours before serving.

Yield: 5 to 6 cups
Total Fat Grams: Less than 1

CUCUMBER SALAD

2 cucumbers, peeled and sliced
1 large onion, sliced into rings
1 cup vinegar
1/2 cup Our Creamy Italian Dressing (page 142)
Freshly ground pepper to taste

Toss the cucumbers and onion rings in large bowl with dressing. Add the vinegar and pepper to taste. Toss well and refrigerate. Serve chilled.

Yield: 4 to 5 cups
Total Fat Grams: 0

KILLER PASTA SALAD

This versatile salad can present a different look with a variety of pasta shapes and colors. For a taste change on this basic recipe, add cold boiled shrimp, poached or grilled chicken, turkey strips, or tuna. Other veggies with those included below will add additional color and flavor as well. Be sure to credit the meal with any fat grams from any seafood or poultry added.

1 pound package egg-free spiral macaroni
1 cup fresh broccoli flowerets
1 cup plain fat-free yogurt
1/4 cup fat-free mayonnaise
2 Tbs. fresh lemon juice
1/2 tsp. pepper
1 clove garlic, minced
1/4 cup green bell pepper, minced
1/2 cup grated carrots
1 Tbs. fresh basil leaves, crushed
1 Tbs. fresh parsley, chopped

Cook pasta until slightly underdone, firm and just tender. Drain and run under cold water until completely cool. Refrigerate. Steam broccoli until crispy-tender, about 3 minutes, and run under cold water until cool. Refrigerate. Blend the yogurt with the mayo and add the lemon juice, pepper and garlic. Toss with all remaining ingredients including pasta and broccoli. Let stand in refrigerator for flavors to meld.

Yield: 7 to 8 cups
Total Fat Grams: 8

PASTA GAZPACHO SALAD

1 3/4 cups crushed tomatoes
1/3 cup onion, chopped
2 cloves garlic, minced
1 Tbs. fresh parsley, chopped
1/2 tsp. sugar
1/2 tsp. chives, chopped
1/2 tsp. basil leaves, chopped
1/2 tsp. hot pepper sauce
12 oz. Garden Style Pasta Twirls (tomato and spinach macaroni)
Olive Oil Pam
2 cups cucumber, diced
1 cup green bell pepper, thinly sliced
1/2 cup celery, sliced

Prepare the dressing by combining tomatoes, onion, garlic, parsley, sugar, chives, basil leaves and hot pepper sauce. Refrigerate. Cook pasta according to package directions and rinse thoroughly with cold water. Toss with a 7 1/2 second spray of Olive Oil Pam. Add vegetables and toss all ingredients with the dressing. Refrigerate until chilled and serve.

Yield: 8 to 9 cups
Total Fat Grams: 10

RED SUNSET SALAD

2 pounds fresh spinach, washed
4 medium tomatoes, ripe but firm
1/4 cup scallions with tops, minced
1 red bell pepper, thinly sliced
1/2 cup cucumber, cubed
1 cup watercress, chopped
6 fresh basil leaves, finely chopped
2 Tbs. fresh lemon juice
Boiling water

Wash and stem the spinach. Place spinach in a colander and pour the boiling water over the spinach. It will reduce in volume and the texture will soften. Drain the spinach. Toss all ingredients in a large bowl and sprinkle with lemon juice. Serve with Jim's Honey Vinaigrette (page 143).

Yield: About 4 cups
Total Fat Grams: Less than 1

CHINESE ASPARAGUS SALAD

15 to 20 fresh asparagus spears, steamed
2 Tbs. rice wine vinegar
1 Tbs. dark brown sugar
1 Tbs. soy sauce
1 tsp. sesame oil
Tomato slices

Cook asparagus until just tender. Cut into 2 inch pieces. Set aside. Prepare the sauce by mixing vinegar, sugar, soy sauce and oil. Toss the asparagus with the sauce and chill. Serve with slices of tomato on top.

Yield: 3 to 4 cups
Total Fat Grams: 5

PICKLED VEGETABLES

2 carrots, sliced
2 celery ribs, sliced
2 cups cauliflower, separated into small pieces
1/2 red bell pepper, thinly sliced
1 green onion including top, sliced
1 clove garlic, sliced
1 cup vinegar
1/2 cup dry white wine
1/4 cup water
1/4 cup apple juice
2 tsp. salt
8 peppercorns
1 tsp. dried dill weed

Mix all ingredients. Place in a glass jar. Close tightly and refrigerate for no less than 24 hours before serving.

Yield: About 5 cups
Total Fat Grams: Less than 1

ANYTIME SUPPER SALAD

The adaptability of this meal-in-a-salad is the advantage of this dish, an all-you-can-eat dinner, with the vegetables offered below as examples of a typical salad which you may feel free to render totally untypical by adding leftover cooked beans or canned red kidney or garbanzo beans, pickles or pickled vegetables, waterpack artichoke hearts, mushrooms, corn, or any frozen vegetable, thawed by running under water and draining. For a heartier dinner, add leftover or canned seafood or poultry. Be sure to add any fat grams from the seafood or poultry you include in this salad. The base of the salad is a combination of any lettuces you choose for color and texture such as romaine, radiccio, leaf lettuce, escarole, or spinach leaves. Use a fat-free dressing of your choice to tie the flavors of your concoction together, and enjoy.

2 cups assorted lettuces
1/2 cup shredded cabbage, red or white
2 celery ribs, sliced
1/2 medium green bell pepper, sliced
1/2 medium red bell pepper, sliced
1/2 cucumber, sliced
1/2 cup thawed, frozen peas
1/2 cup thawed, frozen broccoli flowerets
1/2 cup beans, any variety, cooked or canned
1 Tbs. radish, thinly sliced
1/4 medium Bermuda onion, thinly sliced

Toss all ingredients along with any additions you make on your own. Add the fat-free salad dressing and toss again.

Yield: About 5 cups, without additional vegetables
Total Fat Grams: 1 to 2, if no seafood or poultry added

TACO SALAD

2 cups head lettuce
2 celery ribs, sliced
1/2 medium green bell pepper
1/2 cup Bean Dip (page 113)
1/2 cup Chili Con Queso (page 112) or grated fat-free cheddar
1/2 cup chopped tomato
Baked corn tortilla chips

Place lettuce, celery and green pepper in a salad bowl. Heat the Bean Dip to room temperature. Place over the salad stuff. Heat the Chili Con Queso so that it is melted enough to spoon over the beans. Top with the tomato and garnish with the tortilla chips.

Yield: About 6 cups
Total Fat Grams: 2

ZUCCHINI AND BROCCOLI SALAD

1/2 pound broccoli
2 zucchini, sliced
1 Tbs. vegetable stock or broth
3 Tbs. red wine vinegar
1/4 tsp. dried tarragon
3/4 tsp. dried dill weed
Salt
Freshly ground black pepper
Crisp lettuce leaves
2 crisp red apples, sliced
2 Tbs. fresh lemon juice
1 cup cold water
Parsley sprigs

Break broccoli into flowerets. Thinly slice the stems. Add broccoli stems and zucchini to a large pan with the vegetable stock. Cook until hot and still crunchy, about 1 to 2 minutes. Add the flowerets and cook about 1 minute more. Remove from the heat and stir in vinegar, tarragon and dill weed. Season to taste with salt and pepper. Refrigerate until chilled. Place the sliced apples in a bowl with the water and lemon juice to cover. Arrange the lettuce leaves on plates, drain the chilled broccoli and zucchini and place on the lettuce leaves. Drain the apple slices and arrange on each salad. Garnish with the parsley.

Yield: 4 plates as a salad appetizer
Total Fat Grams: Traces

BLACK AND WHITE BEAN SALAD

1 can (15 oz.) black beans
1 can (15 oz.) white beans
2 jars (7 oz. ea.) roasted peppers
1/2 cup green onions, thinly sliced
1/4 tsp. garlic powder
6 Tbs. white wine vinegar
1 tsp. paprika
1 tsp. chili powder
1 tsp. vegetable oil

Rinse the beans in cold water and drain. Place in bowl and set aside. In blender or food processor, combine the rest of the ingredients and blend. Puree until smooth. Toss the beans with 1 cup of the sauce. Cover and marinate at room temperature for at least 30 minutes and be sure to serve within a time frame of 2 hours.

Yield: 4 cups
Total Fat Grams: 7

BEAN, RICE AND PEA SALAD

2 cups cooked long grain rice
2 cups canned black beans, drained
1 box (10 oz.) frozen petite peas, thawed
1 tsp. olive oil
1/4 cup pimientos, chopped
2 Tbs. ketchup
1 tsp. Dijon mustard
1/4 cup red wine vinegar
Freshly ground black pepper

Place rice, beans and peas in a bowl. Set aside. In a blender or food processor, blend together the rest of the ingredients seasoning with black pepper to taste, and toss with the rice and bean mixture. Cover and chill for 2 hours or more before serving.

Yield: About 6 cups
Total Fat Grams: 7

TABBOULEH-STUFFED TOMATOES

1/2 cup bulgur
1/3 cup scallions, finely chopped
1/4 cup radishes, minced
1/3 cup raisins
1/4 cup fresh lemon juice
2 1/2 second spray of Olive Oil Pam
Salt and freshly ground pepper
4 large tomatoes
1/4 cup fresh parsley, minced

Place bulgur in a medium bowl. Add boiling water to cover by 1 inch. Cover and let stand 1 hour or until water is absorbed. Place bulgur in clean towel. Roll up and squeeze to remove excess water. Transfer the bulgur to a medium bowl and fluff with a fork. Add green onions, radishes, raisins, lemon juice, and spray with Olive Oil Pam. Season to taste with salt and pepper. Cover and let stand for 30 minutes.

Cut a thin slice off the top of each tomato. Scoop out the tomato pulp, chop with tops and add to the bulgur mixture. Mix well. Lightly salt the tomato shells and turn upside down on paper towels to drain for 30 minutes. Blot the insides of the shells with toweling and fill the tomato shells with the bulgur mixture, pressing in firmly. Place stuffed tomatoes on steamer rack and cook for about 2 minutes or until the tomatoes are soft but not falling apart. Cool to room temperature. Line plates with lettuce leaves, place stuffed tomatoes on the leaves and garnish with parsley.

Yield: 4 stuffed tomatoes
Total Fat Grams: 2 to 3

WARM POTATO SALAD

6 to 8 small redskin potatoes
1/2 pound young green beans
1 Tbs. white wine vinegar
1 Tbs. fat-free ricotta cheese
1/2 cup plain non-fat yogurt
1/2 tsp. Dijon mustard
1/4 tsp. paprika
Salt and freshly ground pepper
2 green onions, thinly sliced

Place the unpeeled potatoes in a steamer, cover and steam 5 minutes. Add green beans and steam together, covered, 6 to 8 minutes longer or until potatoes are easily pierced with a fork and green beans are crisp-tender. Set aside. Combine cheese, yogurt, mustard and paprika in a blender or food processor and blend until smooth. Season to taste with salt and pepper. Slice the potatoes and place in a large bowl with the green beans. Toss with the white wine vinegar and salt to taste. Add the dressing and toss to mix. Garnish with the green onions. Serve warm.

Yield: 7 to 8 cups
Total Fat Grams: 0

CURRIED SEAFOOD SALAD

1 can (6 1/2 oz.) chunk-style waterpack tuna
1/4 pound (1 cup) cooked, cleaned shrimp
1/2 cup celery, chopped
1/2 cup fat-free mayonnaise
1/8 tsp. Dijon mustard
2 Tbs. fresh lemon juice
2 tsp. curry powder
3 cups cooked rice, cold
2 to 3 Tbs. fat-free French dressing
1/2 cup snipped parsley

Refrigerate tuna and shrimp. Mix together mayonnaise, mustard, lemon juice and curry powder. Toss chilled seafood with celery and mayo mixture. Set aside. Mix the rice with the French dressing and parsley. Place rice mixture on plates. Top with seafood mixture.

Yield: 3 cups rice and 2 cups seafood salad
Total Fat Grams: 5

SHRIMP SALAD NEW ORLEANS

1 cup cooked rice, cold
1/4 pound (1 cup) cooked, cleaned shrimp
3/4 tsp. salt
1 Tbs. fresh lemon juice
1/4 cup green bell pepper, thinly sliced
1 Tbs. scallions, minced
2 Tbs. fat-free French dressing
1 Tbs. stuffed green olives, sliced
1/4 cup cauliflower, diced
1/3 cup fat-free mayonnaise

Combine all ingredients. Serve chilled.

Yield: About 3 cups
Total Fat Grams: 5

SALAD DRESSINGS

OUR CREAMY ITALIAN DRESSING

This dressing will become a valuable staple in the refrigerator for use with salads, as a dip for vegetables or seafood nibbles.

1 cup fat-free mayonnaise
1/2 cup red wine vinegar
1 packet Good Seasons Italian Dressing dry ingredients

Stir the mayonnaise to make it smooth. Gradually add the vinegar, stirring as you do. Add the dry seasonings and mix well. Add more vinegar if mixture is too thick for your taste. It will thicken in the refrigerator and can be thinned with vinegar or water before use. Keep the dressing stored in the refrigerator.

Yield: About 1 1/2 cups
Total Fat Grams: 0

JIM'S HONEY VINAIGRETTE

When Jim put this marvelous dressing together it was meant for cucumbers. Use it on Red Sunset Salad (page 130), with cucumbers and onions, as a marinade, or as a tasty dressing for seafood or greens.

1 cup fat-free Italian salad dressing
1/4 cup honey
Pinch of ground nutmeg
Pinch of paprika
1 Tbs. Dijon mustard

Combine all ingredients. Refrigerate.

Yield: 1 1/4 cups
Total Fat Grams: 0

SOUR CREAM DRESSING

1/2 cup fat-free sour cream
1 Tbs. onion, minced
1 tsp. sugar
1 Tbs. vinegar
1/2 tsp. bottled capers
1/4 tsp. paprika
1/2 tsp. salt

Combine all ingredients and refrigerate.

Yield: 3/4 cup
Total Fat Grams: 0

THOUSAND ISLAND DRESSING

1/2 cup fat-free cottage cheese
2 Tbs. plain non-fat yogurt
2 Tbs. fat-free mayonnaise
2 Tbs. ketchup
Dash hot pepper sauce
1 Tbs. skim milk
1 Tbs. dill pickle, chopped
Freshly ground pepper

Combine all ingredients except pickle and pepper. Blend thoroughly. Add the pickle. Season to taste with pepper. Keep refrigerated.

Yield: About 1 cup
Total Fat Grams: Less than 1

REMOULADE SAUCE

This dressing which originated in New Orleans is wonderful on seafood as a sauce, as a dip for boiled shrimp, or as a salad dressing.

1 cup fat-free mayonnaise
1/2 cup vinegar
1/2 cup Dijon mustard
1/2 cup ketchup
3 Tbs. prepared horseradish or to taste
1 clove garlic, pureed
1 tsp. Tobasco or hot pepper sauce

Combine all ingredients. Keep refrigerated.

Yield: About 2 1/2 cups
Total Fat Grams: 0

SPICY COCKTAIL SAUCE

This is the king of seafood sauces. It is easy to prepare and never-fail. Adjust the horseradish and Tobasco to suite your own taste.

1 cup bottled chili sauce
2 Tbs. prepared horseradish or to taste
1 Tbs. fresh lemon juice
Tobasco or hot pepper sauce to taste

Combine all ingredients. Keep refrigerated.

Yield: About 1 cup
Total Fat Grams: 0

TARTAR SAUCE

1 cup fat-free mayonnaise
1 Tbs. pickle relish, or minced pickle
1 Tbs. parsley, minced
1 Tbs. bottled capers
1 Tbs. onion, minced

Combine all ingredients. Keep refrigerated.

Yield: About 1 cup
Total Fat Grams: 0

SALSA

This salsa is great alongside any of the Tex-Mex dishes. For speed and ease, however, you'll love Old El Paso Salsa or Pace. The salsas are delicious...and they do all the work!

1 can whole tomatoes (28 oz.) chopped, with juice
1 can (8 oz.) tomato sauce
1 can (4 oz.) diced green chiles
1/2 cup onion, diced
1/2 cup celery, diced
1 Tbs. sugar
1 tsp. salt
Season with onion and garlic powders to taste
Pickled jalapeño peppers, chopped, to taste
White vinegar to taste

Combine all ingredients. Refrigerate for at least 2 hours, taste and correct seasonings, before serving.

Yield: About 6 cups
Total Fat Grams: 0

Soups, Stocks & Gravies

The soups of the world are enjoyed for flavor and versatility, serving as appetizer, lunch, or a meal-in-a-bowl. Every nationality has its well-known version of this wonderful dish from Minestrone, Greek Lentil Soup, French Potato Soup to Scotch Broth. You'll find these on the next pages to help warm your heart on a cold winter's eve and yes, the old-fashioned Jewish Mother's Chicken Soup to soothe you when you have a cold.

Most home-made soups taste better after having been refrigerated overnight which gives the flavors a chance to meld. If there is any fat in the soup it should rise to the top and congeal, facilitating removal before reheating. If you choose to eat one of the many delicious canned soups available, place the soup can in the refrigerator, before opening, for at least four hours, to allow the fat to congeal on top. When you open the can remove the fat first. If you measure the fat you can deduct 4 1/2 grams of fat for each undiluted teaspoonful you remove. If there is a bit of soup mixed in with the fat, deduct 2 1/2 grams of fat per teaspoon from the total gram count listed on the can label.

You'll find an expanding array of low-fat soups on the shelves. Since Campbell's introduction of their new line,

"Healthy Request," using Cream of Mushroom soup for concocting wonderful, fast casserole dishes is a possibility again. The original soup had 19 1/4 grams of fat in the can, undiluted. The "Healthy Request" version has 5 1/2 grams of fat. While my kids were young, those casseroles filled many a schoolnight's menu.

You'll find Progresso has a line of soups called Healthy Classics that are superb, and they have added another line of Pasta Soups that, although not marked for low fat, run about 2 grams per serving or 4 grams for the can. This compares with double that amount, or more, in their original products. Healthy Choice soups are right in there in the flavor department and you'll find many other low-fat brands that are tasty and satisfying, as well. Check them out for cooking with, too.

So many dishes call for sautéing to get the vegetables, such as the onions and garlic, softened. Most often this sautéing is accomplished by using a small amount of oil in the bottom of the pan or pot. You'll find, however, that the recipes that follow call for sautéing in defatted stock, bouillon or dry wine. This is to avoid the use of oils, while maintaining the integrity of the flavors in the dish. This procedure may be performed, stove-top, by introducing the stock, bouillon or wine to the pot or pan, adding the onions, garlic or other veggies, cooking until soft and continuing with the recipe; or placing the stock, bouillon or wine with the vegetables in the microwave and cooking on high until the veggies are soft. A bit of water, alone, may be used in the microwave method for softening the vegetables if the other ingredients are not available. Either of these methods may be used successfully whenever sautéing in oil is called for.

Any of the stocks can be frozen in ice cube trays, removed when set up, and placed in freezer bags. This affords easy access and a method of having handy just the amount you need for sautéing. Be sure to label the different stocks if preparing more than one kind.

CHICKEN OR TURKEY STOCK

5 pounds bony chicken or turkey pieces (necks, back, wings)
12 cups (3 quarts) water
2 carrots, cut in chunks
2 medium onions, quartered
1 bay leaf
2 ribs celery, with tops, cut into pieces
2 sprigs parsley
1/4 tsp. thyme leaves
6 whole peppercorns

In a 6 to 8 quart pot, combine all ingredients. bring to a boil over high heat. Cover and simmer for 2 1/2 to 3 hours. Let cool. Strain and discard all solids. Cover and refrigerate. After 24 hours, remove any fat which has congealed on top. Divide stock into small containers for freezing. Leave about 1/2 inch at top of each container for expansion.

Yield: About 2 1/2 to 3 quarts
Total Fat Grams: When properly defatted, only traces

ROASTED TURKEY STOCK

2 medium onions, quartered
4 celery ribs with tops
3 carrots, cut in thirds
1 parsnip, if available
10 whole peppercorns
5 sprigs parsley
3 Tbs. granulated chicken bouillon
1 turkey carcass

Place all ingredients in a large pot. Cover with water using at least 6 to 8 cups. Simmer, uncovered, for 1 hour. The strength of this stock will very depending on the amount of meat left on the bones of the carcass. Continue to simmer for stronger stock. Refrigerate and defat as with Chicken Stock (page 153).

Yield: About 4 to 5 cups
Total Fat Grams: When properly defatted, only traces

FISH STOCK

1/4 cup dry white wine
1 cup onion, minced
1 cup parsley, finely chopped
3 Tbs. fresh lemon juice
4 pounds fish bones, trimmings and heads (lean, mild, white-fleshed fish is preferable)
1 1/2 cups dry white wine
8 cups water

Sauté onions and parsley in wine until soft. Reduce heat to low. Place fish parts over vegetables, add lemon juice and cook 5 minutes, shaking pan occasionally. Add 1 1/2 cups additional wine and water. Simmer, uncovered for 20 to 30 minutes, until liquid is reduced by half. Let cool and strain. May be frozen for 6 months.

Yield: About 5 cups
Total Fat Grams: Less than 1

VEGETABLE STOCK I

Freeze this stock in ice-cube trays for quick and easy use.

8 cups coarsely shredded, lightly-packed greens (spinach, swiss chard, kale or mustard greens)
1 small head cabbage
1 cup lightly packed parsley sprigs
2 large ribs celery with tops, chopped
1 large onion, coarsely chopped
3 large garlic cloves, minced
1 tsp. thyme leaves
1 bay leaf
15 whole peppercorns
12 cups water

In a 6 to 8 quart enamel or stainless steel pot, combine well-washed greens and all other ingredients. Bring to boil over high heat. Reduce heat and simmer, uncovered, for 1 1/2 hours. Let cool. Strain and discard veggies and seasonings. Cover and refrigerate. Will last up to 4 days in the refrigerator. Divide and freeze in small containers for future use.

Yield: About 8 to 9 cups
Total Fat Grams: 0

VEGETABLE STOCK II

6 ribs celery, cut into 1 inch pieces
4 medium carrots, thickly sliced
4 medium tomatoes, quartered
2 onions, coarsely chopped
1 leak, white and green parts, coarsely chopped
6 sprigs parsley
2 bay leaves
10 whole peppercorns, black or white
1/2 cup water
1 bottle (750 ml.) dry white wine
3 1/2 cups water

Combine all vegetables, bay leaves, peppercorns and 1/2 cup water. Cook in large pot, tightly covered, over moderately low heat about 30 to 40 minutes, until vegetables are soft but not brown. Stir in the wine and increase the heat to moderate. Simmer until reduced by half, about 45 minutes. Add 3 1/2 cups water and return to a simmer. Reduce again by half. Strain and discard vegetables. This stock can be frozen for up to 3 months.

Yield: About 2 cups
Total Fat Grams: 1

MUSHROOM CONSOMMÉ

3 Tbs. defatted stock
1/2 medium onion, thinly sliced
1 Tbs. lemon juice
1/4 pound mushrooms, thickly sliced
3 cups vegetable stock or broth
Salt and pepper to taste
2 Tbs. sherry, optional

Sauté onion in 3 Tbs. stock until soft. Add mushrooms and lemon juice. Cook until tender, about 5 minutes. Add additional stock and heat but do not boil. Add sherry just before serving.

Yield: About 4 cups
Total Fat Grams: Less than 1

BARLEY SOUP

1/4 cup whole barley
6 cups water
1 cup carrots, sliced
1/2 cup celery, diced
1/2 cup onions, diced
2 cups canned tomatoes, chopped
1 cup peas
Salt and freshly ground pepper to taste

Cook barley 1 hour in 6 cups of water. Add remaining ingredients and simmer until vegetables are tender and flavors are blended, about 30 to 45 minutes.

Yield: 8 cups
Total Fat Grams: 2

BEAN WITH GARLIC SOUP

1/4 cup white wine or defatted stock
1 onion, chopped
6 garlic cloves, minced
4 carrots, chopped
2 ribs celery, chopped
2 quarts water
1 can (15 or 16 oz.) stewed or crushed tomatoes
1/4 tsp. dried thyme
3 cups white kidney or navy beans, cooked or canned
1 package (10 oz.) French-cut string beans, thawed
2 Tbs. fresh basil, minced or 1/2 tsp. dried basil
Granulated bouillon, chicken or beef, to taste
Pepper to taste

In a large pot combine stock or wine with onion, garlic, carrots and celery. Cook until tender. Add 2 quarts water, tomatoes and thyme. Bring liquid to a boil, reduce to a simmer and cook for 30 minutes. Add beans and basil, bouillon and pepper to taste. If you like a thicker soup, remove 1 cup of the beans, mash and return to the pot.

Yield: Approximately 14 cups
Total Fat Grams: 5

GREENS WITH BEANS SOUP

1/2 cup dry white wine
1 1/2 cups onion, chopped
1 1/2 cups carrot, chopped
1 clove garlic, minced
4 cups water
1 can pinto beans (15 oz.), rinsed and drained
1/4 cup fresh parsley, chopped
1 tsp. chicken bouillon granules
1/2 tsp. dried whole thyme or 1/4 tsp. ground
1/4 tsp. ground red pepper
1 bay leaf
3 cups kale, coarsely chopped
1 tsp. liquid smoke

Sauté onion, carrot and garlic on high heat until crisp-tender. Add water and all ingredients, except the kale and liquid smoke. Bring to a boil and cover. Reduce heat and simmer 10 minutes. Add the kale and liquid smoke and cook an additional 5 minutes. Remove the bay leaf and serve.

Yield: 6 cups
Total Fat Grams: Traces

TOMATO LENTIL SOUP

1 cup uncooked lentils, picked and rinsed
4 cups water
1 medium onion, chopped
3 potatoes, cubed
3 carrots, sliced
1 bay leaf
1 1/2 tsp. dried basil
1 tsp. dried oregano
2 garlic cloves, minced
1 1/2 cups tomatoes, cooked or canned, broken up
1/2 cup chopped raw spinach
Salt to taste

Rinse lentils and place in a 5 to 6 quart pot with water, onion, potatoes, carrots and seasonings. Bring to a boil, lower heat and simmer, covered, 45 minutes to 1 hour, or until lentils are soft and vegetables are tender. Add tomatoes and spinach. Simmer 10 to 15 minutes. Season to taste.

Yield: About 12 cups
Total Fat Grams: 2

LENTIL TOMATO PASTA SOUP

There are 5 different lentil soup recipes for you here. Yes, lentil soup is delicious...it's also very easy to prepare because there's no soaking required prior to cooking.

1/4 cup white wine or defatted stock
1 onion, chopped
4 garlic cloves, minced
2 cups uncooked lentils, picked and rinsed
7 cups water
1 large can (28 oz.) tomatoes, chopped
1 bay leaf
1 dried hot red pepper
1 tsp. dried oregano
1 Tbs. fresh basil or 1 tsp. dried basil
Salt and freshly ground pepper to taste
4 oz. whole wheat noodles, any shape

Sauté onion and 2 garlic cloves in the wine or stock, in a heavy-bottomed soup pot, until the onion is tender. Add the lentils, water, tomatoes and bay leaf and bring to a boil. Add the red pepper, lower the heat to simmer, cover, and cook for 30 minutes. Remove the red pepper and add the remaining garlic. Cook an additional 30 minutes or until the lentils are tender. Add the oregano and basil, and salt and pepper to taste. If the noodles are long, break them up and add to pot about 10 minutes before serving. Cook until the noodles are tender, about 10 minutes.

Yield: About 12 cups
Total Fat Grams: 4

INDIAN LENTIL SOUP

1/4 cup white wine or defatted stock
1 carrot, chopped
1 onion, chopped
1 rib celery, chopped
1 red bell pepper, chopped
1 Tbs. curry powder
1 cup uncooked lentils, picked and rinsed
1 quart water
1 can (15 Oz.) tomatoes
Freshly ground black pepper and salt to taste

In medium saucepan sauté the carrot, onion, celery and bell pepper for about 3 minutes. Stir in curry powder and sauté for about 1/2 minute more. Add lentils, tomatoes and 1 quart water. Bring to a boil. Reduce to a simmer and cook gently, partially covered, for about 45 minutes or until lentils are very soft. Serve as is, seasoned with the freshly ground black pepper and salt to taste.

Yield: About 6 cups
Total Fat Grams: 3

LENTIL AND PEPPER SOUP

1/2 cup white wine or defatted stock
1 tsp. virgin olive oil
3 medium onions, chopped
3 medium carrots, chopped
7 cups defatted stock or broth
8 garlic cloves, chopped
3/4 cup uncooked lentils, picked and rinsed
1/2 cup sherry
2 red bell peppers, thinly sliced
2 green bell peppers, thinly sliced
Salt and freshly ground pepper to taste

Heat the 1/2 cup of wine or stock and the olive oil in a large soup pot, and add the onions, carrots and garlic. Cook, covered, on low to medium heat, until the onions and carrots are soft, stirring occasionally. Add the additional stock or broth and bring the mixture to a boil. Reduce the heat to a simmer, cover, and cook for about 20 minutes. Remove from heat and with a slotted spoon remove only the solids and about 1 cup of the liquid. Puree in a blender or food processor. Return the pureed mixture to the pot. Add lentils, sherry, peppers, salt and pepper to taste. Simmer, partially covered, for about 25 minutes or until lentils are done. Correct seasoning and serve.

Yield: About 12 cups
Total Fat Grams: 8

GREEK LENTIL SOUP

2 cups uncooked lentils, picked and rinsed
8 cups water
3/4 cup onion, chopped
3/4 cup carrot, chopped
1 cup celery, chopped
1 cup raw potato, chopped
2 bay leaves
1/2 tsp. ground cumin
1/2 tsp. garlic powder
Salt to taste
2 tsp. fresh lemon juice
Fat-free sour cream, optional

Place all ingredients, except the lemon juice, in a large pot. Cook over medium heat until the lentils are soft, about 45 minutes. Add lemon juice and serve. A dollop of fat-free sour cream may be used as a garnish on top.

Yield: About 12 cups
Total Fat Grams: 5

BLACK BEAN SOUP

1 pound black beans, picked and rinsed
1 bay leaf
2 quarts water
1 large onion, chopped
3 cloves garlic, minced
1 carrot, chopped
3 ribs celery, chopped
1 green bell pepper, chopped
1 tsp. cumin
2 tsp. oregano
1 tsp. salt
2 Tbs. cider vinegar
1/2 cup dry white wine
3 cups brown rice, cooked
Hot sauce to taste
1 red onion, diced

Wash and soak the beans, overnight. Drain and place in a large pot with the bay leaf and water. Bring to a boil. Reduce the heat and cook until the beans are tender, about 1 1/2 hours. Place onion, garlic, carrot, celery and green pepper in a cup of the soup liquid and cook in a separate saucepan until tender. Add to the soup pot with the seasonings and vinegar. Simmer, covered, for 30 minutes. For a thicker soup, remove about 25 percent of the beans, puree in a blender or food processor, and return to the pot. Add wine and reheat. Serve on a scoop of brown rice with hot sauce and onion as a garnish.

Yield: About 10 cups, not including the rice
Total Fat Grams: 8

EASY-DOES-IT BEAN MINESTRONE

1 can Healthy Request Vegetable Soup, undiluted
1 can Healthy Request Chicken Noodle Soup, undiluted
1 soup can water
1 can (15 oz.) red kidney beans, undrained
1 can (15 oz.) white kidney beans, undrained
1 clove garlic, minced
1/3 cup fresh snipped parsley or 1 Tbs. dried parsley

Combine all ingredients and cook until heated through.

Yield: About 6 cups
Total Fat Grams: 11

ALASKAN THREE BEAN SOUP

This soup requires time and dedication to prepare. Yet once having tasted it, you'll not hesitate to cook it again. It's that good! It can be a meal with a hunk of fat-free French bread. The recipe yields quite a bit of soup and because it's rich and thick, it goes a long way. Don't let this deter you from preparing it. Since it freezes very well, you'll save lots of time when it's a "re-heat" dinner. If you use canned beans, you'll have leftovers to use in salad or to add to other soups.

1/2 cup white wine or defatted stock
3 cups onion, chopped
2 ribs celery, chopped
3 cloves garlic, minced
6 fresh parsley sprigs
1 1/2 tsp. dried thyme
2 bay leaves
6 cups defatted chicken stock or bouillon
1/2 cup navy beans, precooked or canned
1/2 cup black beans, precooked or canned
1/2 cup red beans, precooked or canned
1/2 cup barley
1 green bell pepper, diced
1 red bell pepper, diced
2 tsp. olive oil
1 1/2 tsp. liquid smoke
3 Tbs. sherry
Salt and pepper to taste

Place the onion, carrot, celery and garlic in a pot with 1/2 cup wine or stock and cook over low heat until the vegetables are tender, about 20 minutes. Add the parsley, thyme and bay leaves along with the stock. Drain the beans and add along with the barley to the pot. Bring to a boil, reduce heat, and simmer, partially covered, for 40 minutes. Pour the soup through a strainer and reserve the stock. Discard the bay leaves and parsley. Remove about 25 percent of the bean and vegetable mixture, along with 1 cup of the stock and puree in a blender or food processor. Return the puree to the reserved stock and add extra chicken or vegetable stock or broth until the soup is the desired consistency. Now return the rest of the beans and vegetables to the soup. Sauté the green and red bell peppers in the olive oil over a medium heat about 10 minutes and add to the soup with a slotted spoon. Add the liquid smoke and the sherry. Simmer for about 20 minutes.

Yield: About 12 cups
Total Fat Grams: 15

NAVY BEAN SOUP

2 cups uncooked white pea beans, picked and rinsed
8 cups water
1/4 tsp. black pepper
1 bay leaf
1/2 tsp. salt
2 cups celery, chopped
1 cup carrots, chopped
1 cup onion, chopped
1/2 tsp. garlic powder
1/4 cup parsley, chopped
1 can (8 oz.) tomato sauce
Dash ground cloves, optional

Soak the beans overnight in cold water. Drain. Add 8 cups water, pepper and bay leaf. Bring to a boil, reduce to simmer and cook for about 2 hours or until the beans are tender. Add salt, celery, carrots, onion, garlic, tomato sauce and parsley. Add the cloves, if desired. Simmer for 1 hour. Mash some of the beans to thicken the soup and simmer for another hour.

Yield: About 12 cups
Total Fat Grams: 7

AUNT ROSE'S MINESTRONE

1/4 cup white wine or defatted stock
1 large onion, chopped
2 ribs celery, sliced
1/4 head cabbage, shredded
2 cans (15 oz. ea.) stewed tomatoes
1 tsp. dried mixed Italian seasonings
1 can (10 1/2 oz.) garbanzo beans, with liquid
1 can (7 oz.) whole kernel corn, with liquid
2 zucchini, sliced
1 1/2 tsp. granulated beef or chicken bouillon
1/2 tsp. dried basil
2 1/2 cups defatted chicken broth
3/4 cup small, eggless pasta, uncooked

Sauté onion, celery and cabbage in wine or stock for 3 to 4 minutes. Add all remaining ingredients except the pasta. Bring to a boil and reduce to a simmer. Cook for 30 minutes, stirring occasionally. Add pasta and cook for about 8 to 10 minutes or until the pasta is done.

Yield: About 10 cups
Total Fat Grams: 2

MEREDITH'S MINESTRONE

This soup tastes even better after refrigerating and reheating. It will thicken upon refrigeration and water may be added to return the soup to the lighter consistency.

1/2 cup white wine or defatted stock
1 cup onion, coarse-chop
1 cup carrots, chopped
1 cup celery, chopped
1 cup leek, washed well and chopped
2 cloves garlic, minced
2 cups potatoes, peeled and diced
2 turnips, peeled and diced
2 cups zucchini, diced
1 cup fresh green beans, trimmed and sliced
3 cups cabbage, shredded
2 cups mushrooms, sliced
8 cups defatted chicken broth
1/2 cup frozen peas
1 cup canned plum tomatoes, chopped, with juice
2 cups canned cannellini beans, drained and rinsed
1/2 cup small, eggless pasta, uncooked
Salt and freshly ground black pepper to taste

Sauté the onion in 1/2 cup wine or stock over medium to high heat until tender. Add the carrots and cook for 2 to 3 minutes. Add each vegetable in turn, starting with the carrots and ending with the mushrooms, cooking each vegetable for 2 to 3 minutes, stirring after each addition. Add the soup, peas and tomatoes with juice. Bring to a boil. Reduce heat and simmer, covered, for 2 1/2 hours. Add the cannellini beans and continue cooking for another half-hour. About 8 to 10 minutes before serving, add the pasta.

Yield: About 22 cups
Total Fat Grams: 8

EVERYTHING VEGETABLE SOUP

Now is the time to do your thing! You have *carte blanche* to add whatever vegetables, legumes or starches you have in the pantry or left over in the fridge. The volume of soup you end up with varies according to the number of ingredients you choose to include, so the yield and total fat grams are relative to your additions.

3 to 4 cans (14 1/2 oz. ea.) crushed or whole tomatoes, with juice
2 to 3 cans (15 oz. ea.) tomato sauce
6 ribs celery, with tops, coarse-chopped
2 large onions, coarse-chopped
1 green bell pepper, chopped
1 can (7 oz.) whole kernel corn
1 box (10 oz.) frozen lima beans
1/2 head cabbage, shredded or chopped
1 cup carrots, sliced
2 cloves garlic, minced
1 to 2 cans (16 oz. ea.) red kidney beans
1 can (16 oz.) white kidney beans
1 to 2 cups redskin potatoes, scrubbed and cubed
4 Tbs. granulated beef or chicken bouillon
8 to 12 cups water
2 zucchini, sliced
Worcestershire sauce to taste
Salt and freshly ground pepper to taste
1/2 cup wine, optional

Place all ingredients in a large pot except the zucchini, Worcestershire sauce and seasonings. If you are using whole tomatoes, break them up with a spoon. Add any other vegetables you choose at this time except for pastas which must be added 8 to 10 minutes before serving, to avoid pasty pasta. Rice, if used instead of the potatoes, may be added to the pot, raw, to cook along with the vegetables. Cook until all vegetables are sufficiently tender and the rice is done.

Add the zucchini and cook an additional 10 minutes or until just tender. Add the rest of the ingredients to taste. If you like a thicker soup, some of the beans may be mashed or 3 to 4 tablespoons cornstarch, dissolved in 1/2 cup cold water, may be added. It will take about 10 minutes of cooking time for the starch mixture to thicken the soup.

Yield: This soup varies according to your own additions
Total Fat Grams: Should not exceed 3 to 8 grams, depending on the choice and quantity of beans used

MINESTRONE WITH KALE

This dish is not just a soup. It's a meal in one dish. And, yet, it takes only about 15 minutes to prepare. Many a cold winter's eve has been warmed up with this soup for dinner after a hard day's work. Try it. If you want a heartier soup, add a hunk of smoked turkey sausage and cook it along with the other ingredients. Remember to add the fat grams for the addition according to the label on the sausage package.

2 to 3 cups raw kale
1 can Progresso Healthy Classics Minestrone (16 oz.) or any other canned vegetable or minestrone soup
1 can red kidney beans (15 1/2 oz.)
1 can Great Northern beans (15 1/2 oz.) (optional)
Defatted chicken stock (optional)
Steamed Rice
Hot pepper sauce

Clean the kale and remove the hard stems. Break into bite-size pieces. Place the minestrone in a large saucepan. Add the kale and the beans. The Great Northern beans may be added if you want more volume. They help to change the consistency of the dish and you may end up using them only on occasion and not necessarily all the time. The additional stock is to make the dish soupier and should be determined by individual taste. Without it the dish is more like a stew. Cover and cook until the kale is wilted or soft. Ladle over steamed rice. Add hot pepper sauce to taste.

Yield: Varies depending on brand of soup and quantities of rice, beans and kale.
Total Fat Grams: Only that amount in the soup you choose and about 1 per cup of beans.

GARLIC, POTATO AND CELERY SOUP

1/4 cup defatted stock
1 medium onion, chopped
6 to 8 cloves garlic, peeled and whole
8 to 10 ribs celery, sliced
1 tsp. dried parsley
2 potatoes, peeled and diced
8 to 10 cups water
1 to 2 Tbs. granulated vegetable bouillon
Salt and freshly ground pepper to taste

Sauté onion in stock until tender. Add garlic and celery and cook 2 to 3 minutes. Add remaining ingredients and simmer, covered for 30 minutes. Remove from heat, season to taste and place in a blender or food processor. Puree, return to pot and heat through.

Yield: About 10 cups
Total Fat Grams: Less than 1

FRENCH POTATO SOUP

The benefit of this delicious soup is its versatility, served hot in winter or cold, as Vichyssoise, a hearty yet delicately flavored appetizer for an elegant dinner.

1/4 cup white wine or defatted stock
3 leeks, cleaned and sliced
1 onion, sliced
4 medium potatoes, peeled and thinly sliced
4 cups defatted chicken stock
2 cups skim milk
2 Tbs. Butter Buds
Salt and pepper to taste
Chopped chives or parsley as garnish

Sauté onion and leeks in 1/4 cup wine or stock until tender. Add potatoes and 4 cups chicken stock and simmer until potatoes are very tender. Remove the vegetables and puree in a blender or food processor. Return vegetable puree to the soup. Mix the milk with the butter buds and add to the soup. Cook on low until heated through. Season to taste and eat hot or chill overnight and eat very cold as Vichyssoise. Garnish with chives or parsley before serving, if desired.

Yield: About 8 cups
Total Fat Grams: Less than 1

POTATO, FENNEL AND LEEK SOUP

2 leeks, light green and white parts only
2 Tbs. liquid Butter Buds
1 tsp. olive oil
Chicken stock, if necessary
1 carrot, peeled and chopped
1/2 bulb fennel, trimmed, chopped (3/4 cup)
3 baking potatoes, peeled and cut in chunks
1/2 tsp. dried thyme
2 Tbs. chopped parsley
1 small bay leaf
4 1/2 cups chicken stock
Salt and pepper to taste

In a soup kettle, cook leeks slowly in Butter Buds liquid and oil for 5 minutes. Add a bit of stock if too dry. Add the carrot and fennel and cook 5 minutes more. Add other ingredients and bring to boil. Cover and simmer 25 to 30 minutes or until potato is tender. Discard the bay leaf. Mash 1/3 of the soup in the pot and stir gently to distribute evenly. Season to taste.

Yield: 8 cups
Total Fat Grams: 5

SPLIT PEA SOUP

And you always thought pea soup had to have ham in it to taste good. Wait till you taste this pea soup!

1 pound dry green split peas
5 cups water
4 bay leaves
1 cup onion, chopped
1/2 cup dry white wine
2 cloves garlic, minced
1 tsp. dried thyme
1/2 tsp. dried rosemary, crushed
1 cup carrots, chopped
1 cup celery, chopped
1 cup red bell pepper, chopped
1/2 cup vegetable stock or bouillon
1 Tbs. fresh basil, chopped or 1 tsp. dried
Salt and freshly ground black pepper to taste

Cook the split peas with the bay leaves in the water until most of the water has been absorbed, about 45 minutes. In a large pot sauté the onion in the wine adding the garlic, thyme, rosemary and some of the freshly ground pepper. When the onion is tender, add the carrots and celery. Continue to cook until all the vegetables are tender. Add the red bell pepper and cook for 2 to 3 minutes. Turn off the heat and set aside. When the peas are cooked, remove the bay leaves and run the peas through a blender or food processor. Combine the pureed peas with the other veggies in the pot and stir. Gradually add the stock or bouillon until the consistency is right to you. Some will enjoy a thicker soup. Add the basil, then the salt and pepper to taste.

Yield: About 8 cups
Total Fat Grams: 4

ONION TOMATO SOUP

1/2 cup defatted chicken stock or broth
2 cups onion, thinly sliced
1 can consomme, undiluted and defatted
1 soup can water
1 can tomato soup, undiluted
1 soup can skim milk
1/2 tsp. Worcestershire sauce
Salt and pepper to taste

Sauté the onion in 1/2 cup stock or broth until tender. Add consomme and water. Simmer, covered, 15 minutes. Add the rest of the ingredients and heat thoroughly, but do not boil.

Yield: About 4 cups
Total Fat Grams: 4

TOMATO SOUP WITH BASIL

1/4 cup white wine or defatted stock
1 large onion, sliced
1 medium carrot, shredded
4 large ripe tomatoes, peeled, seeded and coarsely chopped (about 4 cups)
1/2 cup fresh basil, packed
1 tsp. salt
3/4 tsp. sugar
1/8 tsp. white pepper
2 cups defatted chicken stock or broth
1 Tbs. tiny pasta for soup

Sauté the onion and carrot in the wine or stock until the onion is soft. Stir in the tomatoes, basil, salt, sugar and pepper. Increase the heat to medium-high and bring to a boil, stirring constantly. Reduce heat and cover. Simmer for 10 minutes. Blend the tomato mixture, a small portion at a time, in a food processor or blender, just until smooth. Set aside. Pour stock or broth into pot and bring to a boil. Add soup pasta and cook until tender, about 7 minutes. Stir in the tomato mixture and heat until steaming.

Yield: About 6 cups
Total Fat Grams: 1 to 2

VEGETABLE SOUP WITH BASIL

1/2 cup white wine or defatted stock
1 medium onion, chopped
1/2 cup celery, coarsely chopped
1 medium carrot, sliced
1 large russet potato, peeled and cut into 1-inch slices
2 large tomatoes, peeled and diced
6 cups defatted chicken stock or broth
1/2 tsp. salt
1/8 tsp. pepper
2 Tbs. fresh basil, chopped or 1 tsp. dried basil
1/2 small head cauliflower, broken into flowerets
1/4 pound green beans, cut into 2-inch pieces
2 small zucchini, sliced
1 package (10 oz.) frozen peas
1 cup cabbage, shredded

Sauté the onion, celery and carrot in 1/2 cup wine or stock, in a large soup pot, until soft, about 10 minutes. Add potato, tomatoes, remaining stock, salt, pepper and basil. Bring to a boil. Reduce heat and simmer, covered, for about 20 minutes. Add cauliflower and green beans and simmer another 10 minutes. Add peas and cabbage and simmer another 5 minutes or until all vegetables are tender.

Yield: About 12 cups
Total Fat Grams: 3

JEWISH MOTHER'S CHICKEN SOUP

This is the real thing, also known as "Jewish penicillin."

1 whole stewing chicken, skinned
2 large onions, quartered
6 ribs celery with tops, cut in large pieces
4 carrots, cut in large pieces
1 parsnip, cut in large pieces
1 Tbs. whole black peppercorns
6 sprigs fresh parsley
1 large piece cheesecloth
Salt and pepper to taste
Dill weed, fresh or dried, to taste

Clean poultry and place the whole bird, along with the neck and giblets, in a large pot in water to cover. Place all other ingredients, except the salt, pepper and dill weed, in the cheesecloth and tie off. Place in the pot with the chicken. The cheesecloth will facilitate removal of these vegetables when the soup is done. Add 1 Tbs. salt to the water and boil. Reduce to a simmer, and cook, uncovered, until the meat falls off the bone when touched with a fork, about 1 1/2 hours. Add salt, pepper and dill weed to taste. Continue to simmer the soup, uncovered, until the flavor meets your expectations. Set chicken aside to use in salad or sandwiches. Refrigerate the soup for 6 hours or so for ease in defatting. The meat may be replaced in the soup with some of the cooked carrots from the cheesecloth, and cooked rice or noodles, before serving.

Yield: About 6 to 8 cups
Total Fat Grams: Broth, 1 to 2 grams, if defatted properly. Meat, varies depending on whether white or dark meat is consumed. White = 1 gram per oz., Dark = 2 1/2

SCOTCH BROTH

4 cups cabbage, shredded
2 white turnips, peeled and cut into 1-inch chunks
2 carrots, cut into 1-inch pieces
1 Tbs. sugar
4 cloves garlic, minced
3/4 cup pearled barley
2 quarts defatted chicken broth or bouillon
1 package (10 oz.) frozen peas, thawed
1 pound cooked, skinned turkey breast, cut into 1-inch cubes
Freshly ground pepper and dill weed to taste

Place the first 6 ingredients in a large pot with the chicken broth or bouillon. Bring to a boil and reduce to a simmer. Cover and cook gently for about 1 1/2 hours. Retain liquid at same level in the pot by adding water if necessary. Add peas and turkey and simmer for 10 minutes. Add pepper and dill weed.

Yield: About 12 cups
Total Fat Grams: 6

CIOPPINO

1/4 cup white wine or defatted stock
1 large onion, chopped
2 cloves garlic, minced
1 green bell pepper, chopped
1/3 cup parsley, chopped
1 large can (16 oz.) tomato sauce
1 large can (28 oz.) tomatoes, with juice
1 cup dry red or dry white wine
1 bay leaf
1 tsp. dried basil leaves
1/2 tsp. dried oregano leaves
12 small, hard shell clams, scrubbed
1 pound medium shrimp, cleaned and deveined
2 to 4 large hard-shell crabs, cleaned and cracked

Sauté onion, garlic, bell pepper and parsley in 1/4 cup wine or stock, until the onion is soft. Stir in the tomato sauce, tomatoes (break them up with a spoon) and the liquid, 1 cup wine, bay leaf, basil and oregano. Bring to a boil. Then reduce heat, cover and simmer for 20 minutes. Add clams, shrimp and crabs. Cover and cook for about 8 to 10 minutes or until shells are opened and shrimp turn pink. Discard any unopened clam shells.

Yield: About 12 cups
Total Fat Grams: 20

MANHATTEN CLAM CHOWDER

2 Tbs. white wine or defatted stock
1 tsp. dried thyme
1 cup onion, sliced
3 cups potatoes, peeled and cubed
1/2 cup celery, diced
5 cups hot water
2 tsp. salt
3 1/2 cups canned tomatoes
1 1/2 cups carrots, diced
3 cups clam liquid or broth
2 cups chopped or baby clams, canned
1 Tbs. parsley, snipped
1/2 tsp. dried thyme
Freshly ground pepper to taste

Sauté onion with 1 tsp. thyme in 2 Tbs. wine or stock. Add potatoes, celery, water and salt. Simmer, covered, for 5 minutes. Add tomatoes, carrots and clam liquid and simmer, uncovered, over very low heat, for 1 hour. Add the clams to the soup with the parsley and 1/2 tsp. dried thyme. Simmer, uncovered, 10 minutes. Season with pepper and additional salt to taste.

Yield: About 12 cups
Total Fat Grams: 8

EASY ITALIAN FISH SOUP

3 Tbs. white wine or defatted stock
1 large onion, chopped
1/2 green bell pepper, chopped
2 cloves garlic, minced
1 can (10 oz.) tomato soup, undiluted
1 can (10 oz.) stewed tomatoes
1 can (19 oz.) Progresso Manhatten Clam Chowder
1 Tbs. oregano leaves, crushed
1 tsp. granulated chicken bouillon
1 pound frozen cod fillets, cut in big cubes
1 bay leaf
1 pound shrimp, cleaned and deveined
1 can (6 1/2 oz.) baby clams or chopped clams
1/4 cup white wine (optional)
Hot sauce

Sauté onion, bell pepper and garlic in 3 Tbs. wine or stock, until tender. Add all other ingredients except clams, shrimp and additional wine. Simmer 10 minutes, covered. Add clams, shrimp and wine. Simmer 15 minutes more or until shrimp are cooked through.

Yield: About 8 cups
Total Fat Grams: 18

BAHAMIAN FISH CHOWDER

3 pounds grouper, skinned, boned and cut into 1/2 inch cubes
3/4 cup lime juice
1 green bell pepper, diced
3 ribs celery, diced
1/2 cup white wine or defatted stock
1 large onion, diced
1 tsp. dried thyme
4 cups canned tomatoes
1 can (6 oz.) tomato paste
4 potatoes, peeled and diced
1/4 cup Worcestershire sauce
1 1/2 tsp. liquid smoke
Freshly ground pepper to taste

Marinate the fish cubes in just 1/2 cup lime juice with a little salt and pepper for 1 hour. In a large pot, partially cook the fish in 1/2 cup of wine or stock. Remove the fish and set aside. Add the onion, green pepper and celery to the pot and cook until soft. Add the thyme, tomatoes, tomato paste and potatoes with the liquid smoke and simmer for 1 hour. Add the fish and cook for 20 minutes or until done. Add the Worcestershire sauce and the remaining lime juice just before serving.

Yield: About 12 cups
Total Fat Grams: 6

THICK MUSHROOM GRAVY

1/4 cup dry white wine
1 medium onion, sliced
1/2 pound mushrooms, sliced
1 Tbs. dried parsley
2 cups defatted stock
2 Tbs. cornstarch dissolved in 1/4 cup cold water

Sauté the onion in the wine until soft. Add the mushrooms and parsley and cook over low heat until mushrooms are tender. Add the stock. When the liquid is bubbling, add the cornstarch mixture and stir until thickened.

Yield: 2 to 3 cups
Total Fat Grams: 0

CREAMY MUSHROOM GRAVY

1/4 cup dry white wine or defatted stock
1 medium onion, thinly sliced
1/2 pound mushrooms, sliced
1 can Healthy Request Cream of Mushroom Soup, undiluted
1/2 cup defatted stock

Sauté the onion in 1/4 cup wine or stock, until tender. Add mushrooms and cook over low heat for about 5 minutes. Stir the soup and 1/2 cup stock, thoroughly, to avoid lumps and add to mushroom and onion mixture. Cook over medium heat until heated through.

Yield: 2 to 3 cups
Total Fat Grams: 6

GIBLET GRAVY

1 chicken or turkey neck, skinned
Giblets from a turkey or chicken, rinsed
1 medium onion, chopped
1 rib celery, minced
1 Tbs. granulated chicken bouillon
2 cups water
1 Tbs. cornstarch dissolved in 1/4 cup water

Place all ingredients, except the cornstarch, in a medium saucepan. Add more water, if necessary, to cover. Cook over medium heat until the giblets are tender, about 45 minutes. Remove giblets, mince and return to the pot. Remove the neck, pick the meat off the bones and add the meat back to the pot. Discard the bones. Cook an additional 10 minutes. Add the cornstarch mixture and stir until thickened.

Yield: About 3 cups
Total Fat Grams: 2

BEANS, RICE & PASTA

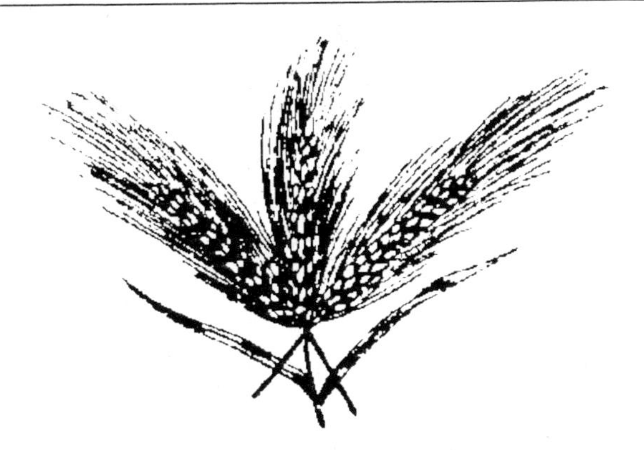

This whole category of recipes features foods long considered forbidden to people trying to stay trim. Now, with your new knowledge of the healthful benefits of complex carbohydrates you can enjoy these foods and the robust satisfaction they deliver. These noble dishes will open a new world of gastronomic pleasures: the magic of the bean and with it the fun of pastas and grains. You will be amazed at the ease of preparation and, best of all, the variety of flavors and textures.

Dried beans can be prepared from scratch or you can purchase beans ready-to-eat. The only difference you'll encounter in taste is the additional salt in the canned beans for which you must make allowances when following any recipe. The major difference between the dried and canned beans is the cost. The dried beans are a much better buy. Make the comparison yourself, keeping in mind the dried beans double in volume when cooked. There are occasions when time will not allow for the soaking and cooking of the dried beans and the canned variety will serve in good stead. It's a good idea to have a few of your favorites on hand for a quick dinner. And since beans, rice and pasta freeze very well, leftovers can make an attractive microwave dinner.

If you decide to prepare the dried beans from scratch and you're not sure how to freeze them after cooling, since different recipes call for varying amounts, here's a nifty way to freeze beans and have the correct amount ready at a moment's notice. Place the cooled beans in a large freezer-proof plastic bag. Squeeze out the air and seal the bag. Lay the bag flat on a table or counter-top and distribute the beans evenly over the bag so you have a wide, flat distribution of beans in the bag. Place in the freezer so that the bag freezes like a board. When you're ready for some beans (and this method works for rice, as well) hold the end of this frozen slab and gently hit on the end of a table. The bean slab will break into frozen pieces which you can then remove and use in any recipe or thaw for use in a salad, taking only the amount you want from the bag at any time.

HOW TO PREPARE DRIED BEANS :
Although lentils, split peas and blackeye peas fall into the legume family, they do not require precooking or soaking. The following instructions apply to the other varieties of bean.

Always pick through the beans and peas for any undesirable foreign material such as small stones. Rinse the beans well. Place in a large, deep pot. Add enough water to cover the beans by 2 inches. The beans are now ready to soak utilizing either the slow or the quick method. Both work equally well. The slow method: soak, covered, overnight, or, for at least 6 to 8 hours. The quick method: bring to a boil and boil for 2 minutes, remove from heat, cover, and let stand for 1 hour.

After soaking, follow these instructions for cooking: drain and cover in fresh water about 1 to 2 inches above the beans and cook for about 30 minutes to 1 hour, or until the beans are tender. Some beans take longer than others. Never add salt or acidic ingredients such as tomatoes, vinegar or lemon juice to the water because these additives will stop the tenderizing action and the beans will not soften. Many a good pot of beans has ended up in the disposal because of a teaspoon of salt. You are now ready to continue with any recipe calling for cooked or canned beans.

It's the time to experiment with an open mind and heart. Remember, if you have a problem with flatulence, the product Beano is available in your drugstore and can help eliminate this discomfort. So jump into the bean and get to know your grains and pastas that are so low in fat and high in nutrition.

JIM'S BEANS

These are Jim's famous Arkansas pinto beans. We cook them up, package them in meal-sized freezer bags, and always have them ready to defrost and serve with Red Rice (page 224) and corn. It's a touch of heaven.

8 cups pinto beans, cooked
1 large onion, chopped
1 green bell pepper, chopped
1/4 to 1/2 cup pickled jalapeño slices, optional
1 can (14 1/2 oz.) whole or stewed tomatoes, with juice
1 Tbs. liquid smoke
Salt and pepper to taste
Hot sauce or salsa to taste

Place beans with liquid in a large pot along with all other ingredients. Cook over medium-low heat for 1 1/2 hours. Adjust seasonings to taste. Serve on brown rice or Red Rice (page 224) Also great in a pita pocket with salsa.

Yield: About 10 to 12 cups
Total Fat Grams: 4

SPICY BAKED BEANS

2 cans (15 oz. ea.) dark red kidney beans
1 can (16 oz.) black beans
1 can (16 oz.) white kidney beans
1 large can (28 oz.) plum tomatoes, drained and chopped
1 cup onion, chopped
2 cloves garlic, minced
1/4 cup dark molasses
1/4 cup cider vinegar
2 Tbs. light clover honey
2 tsp. dried oregano
2 tsp. dry mustard
2 tsp. ground cumin
1 1/2 tsp. ground ginger
1 tsp. chili powder
1/8 tsp. red pepper flakes
Salt to taste

Rinse and drain beans. Place in an oven-proof casserole dish. Add the remaining ingredients and combine, gently, with the beans. Bake, covered, at 350° for 45 minutes. Remove cover, stir and continue baking, uncovered, for an additional 30 minutes or until hot and bubbly.

Yield: About 12 cups
Total Fat Grams: 10

CANNELLINI BEANS AND ONIONS

1/4 cup white wine
2 cups cooked or canned cannellini beans
1 medium onion, sliced
1 to 2 tsp. garlic powder
1/4 cup white wine, additional
Hot sauce to taste

Soften onion in 1/4 cup white wine. Add the beans and remaining ingredients and cook until heated through.

Yield: About 2 cups
Total Fat Grams: 2

CANNELLINI BEAN, SPINACH, RICE CASSEROLE

This dish is an expanded version of the recipe on page 198. The additional veggies enhance the delicate flavor of the beans.

3/4 cup defatted chicken broth
1 large carrot, thinly sliced
2 tsp. powdered garlic
1 medium onion, thinly sliced
1 stalk celery, thinly sliced
1 box frozen spinach leaves, thawed
2 cups cannellini beans, cooked or canned
1/2 cup dry white wine
4 oz. sliced pimentos, drained
3 cups steamed rice
Hot sauce to taste

Soften the carrot, sprinkled with garlic, in the broth. Add the onion, celery, and spinach. Cook until the onion and celery are soft. Add the beans, wine, pimentos and toss. Add the rice, heat through and serve with hot sauce to taste.

Yield: About 6 cups
Total Fat Grams: 3

CANNELLINI WITH TOMATOES

1/4 cup white wine or defatted stock
2 cloves garlic, minced
1 cup onion, chopped
1 1/2 cups tomatoes, chopped
1 tsp. dried parsley
1 can (19 oz.) cannellini or 2 cups cooked
Salt and pepper to taste

Sauté onion and garlic in wine or stock. Add tomatoes and seasonings and simmer 5 minutes. Add beans and heat through. Add salt and pepper to taste.

Yield: About 4 cups
Total Fat Grams: 2

CURRIED BEAN AND EGGPLANT

2 cups canned or cooked white kidney beans, with liquid
1 medium eggplant (about 1 to 1 1/2 pounds), cut into 1-inch cubes
2 carrots, sliced
1 onion, thinly sliced
2 tsp. curry powder
1 tsp. ground cumin
1/4 cup water
1 Tbs. fresh lemon juice
Freshly ground pepper to taste

Place all ingredients, except the lemon juice, in a large pot. Cover and simmer gently for 45 minutes or until eggplant is tender. Drain off the liquid and place in another pot in which you will cook the liquid down to 1/2 cup. Add back to the eggplant mixture. Add lemon juice and salt and pepper to taste.

Yield: About 6 cups
Total Fat Grams: 5

BEANS AND ZUCCHINI

1/4 cup white wine or defatted stock
1 large onion, chopped
1 medium red bell pepper, chopped
1 cup red beans, canned and drained
1 cup white beans, canned and drained
1 cup chickpeas (garbanzo beans), canned and drained
1 can (8 oz.) tomato sauce
1/2 tsp. celery seed
1 small zucchini, cut in 3/4 inch dice
1 small yellow summer squash, cut in 3/4 inch dice
Freshly ground black pepper to taste

In a medium saucepan sauté the onion and red pepper in the wine or stock until tender. Add the beans, tomato sauce and celery seed. Cover and simmer for 15 minutes. Mix in squashes and simmer, covered, for about 5 minutes or until the squash is crisp-tender.

Yield: About 8 cups
Total Fat Grams: 4

CHICKPEA MAC

1 1/2 cups uncooked small shell macaroni or 2 cups uncooked large macaroni
1/4 cup white wine or defatted stock
1 medium onion, chopped
1 can (16 oz.) tomatoes with juice
1 can (16 oz.) chickpeas (garbanzo beans), drained
2 Tbs. fresh parsley, chopped
1 tsp. ground cumin
Salt and pepper to taste

Cook macaroni according to package directions. Drain in colander and set aside. Sauté the onion in the wine or stock until tender. Add chickpeas and tomatoes with juice, breaking up the tomatoes with a spoon. Simmer, uncovered, for 10 minutes. Add macaroni and mix with tomatoes and beans. Add seasonings and simmer an additional 4 minutes.

Yield: About 8 cups
Total Fat Grams: 3

QUICK CHILI BEANS

2 cans (15 oz.) Old El Paso Mexe-Beans
1 medium onion, sliced
1 medium green bell pepper, sliced
Salsa to taste

Combine all ingredients. Cook until veggies are tender. Serve on Red Rice or in fat-free tortillas with salsa.

Yield: About 4 cups
Total Fat Grams: 4

VEGETARIAN CHILI

This recipe is not a quick fix! It takes time to clean, cut and measure all these ingredients. But is it ever worth it! Once the cutting is done, though, it literally cooks itself. It's another one you can separate and freeze for a quickly defrosted meal in a bowl.

1/4 cup white wine
1 large onion, chopped
4 cloves garlic, minced
1/2 pound mushrooms, chopped
2 cups frozen cauliflower pieces
1 large potato. peeled, diced large
1 large green bell pepper, chopped
2 large carrots, chopped
3 cups corn kernels
1 can plum tomatoes (28 oz.), chopped, include juice
1 pound dried kidney beans, soaked and cooked or 1 large can (52 oz.)
1 cup Bloody Mary Mix or other spiced tomato juice
1 Tbs. cumin
2 Tbs. Chili powder
1 tsp. paprika
1 1/2 tsp. salt
1/8 tsp. ground red pepper
2 Tbs. tomato paste
3 Tbs. dry red wine

Sauté the onion and garlic in the wine for about 5 minutes. Add mushrooms and cook for 10 minutes. Stir in everything else and bring to a boil. Reduce to simmer and cook, covered, for about 30 minutes or until the veggies are done. May be served over Red Rice.

Yield: 10 to 12 cups
Total Fat Grams: 6

EASY BEAN GUMBO

1 1/2 cups frozen okra
1/4 cup white wine or defatted stock
1 cup onion, chopped
2 cloves garlic, mashed
1/2 cup celery, diced
1 medium green bell pepper, chopped
2 cans (16 oz. ea.) tomatoes
Dash Cayenne pepper or hot pepper sauce to taste
1 tsp. thyme leaves
1 cup frozen peas
1 can (16 oz.) kidney beans, drained
Salt and pepper, and hot pepper sauce to taste

Cook okra in boiling water or thaw in microwave until tender. Set aside. Sauté onion and garlic in the wine or stock until onion is soft. Add celery and green pepper and cook until tender. Add tomatoes and heat until boiling. Reduce heat and add cayenne and thyme. Simmer 45 minutes. Add cooked okra, peas and beans. Cook until peas are done. Do not overcook the vegetables. Season with salt, pepper and hot pepper sauce.

Yield: About 6 cups
Total Fat Grams: 2

SOUTH OF THE BORDER IN A POT

1/2 cup white wine or defatted stock
1 1/2 cups onion, chopped
2 medium green bell peppers, chopped
1 can (16 oz.) kidney beans
2 cans (16 oz. ea.) pinto beans
1 can (16 oz.) tomatoes with juice
1 tsp. oregano leaves
1/2 tsp. ground cumin
1 tsp. sage
3/4 tsp. pepper

Sauté the onion and green pepper in the wine or stock. Drain the beans and reserve the liquid. Combine all ingredients and place in a 3-quart casserole. Add enough of the reserved liquid to cover the beans (about 1/2 cup). Bake at 375° for 1 hour. Season to taste.

Yield: About 8 cups
Total Fat Grams: 5

RICE AND BEANS ITALIANO

1/2 cup white wine or defatted stock
2 cloves garlic, minced
1 large onion, chopped
2 carrots, chopped
1 large green bell pepper, chopped
1 rib celery, chopped
2/3 cup fresh parsley, chopped, or 1/4 cup dried parsley
3 Tbs. fresh basil, chopped, or 1 tsp. dried basil
1 tsp. oregano
3 large tomatoes, chopped, or 2 cups canned tomatoes, drained
2 cups canned kidney beans, drained
5 cups cooked rice
Salt and pepper to taste
Flaked red pepper to taste

Sauté the garlic, onion, carrots, green pepper and celery in the wine or stock until tender. Add the parsley, basil and oregano. Combine tomatoes, beans and rice in a large, heavy skillet. Season with salt and pepper and the red pepper flakes, if desired. Toss together and heat through. may be served with a sprinkle of Parmesan cheese, but remember to add the extra 1 gram of fat per tablespoon, which is not included in the fat-gram count below, or use Weight Watchers Fat Free Parmesan Cheese.

Yield: About 10 cups
Total Fat Grams: 3

SOUTHERN BLACKEYE PEAS

2 cans (16 oz. ea.) blackeye peas
Olive Oil Pam
1 medium onion, thinly sliced
1/4 tsp. cayenne pepper
1/4 tsp. liquid smoke

Sauté the onion in the Pam until transparent. Add 1 tablespoon defatted stock to the pan if the onions are sticking. Add peas, liquid smoke and cayenne pepper and cook over medium heat for 10 minutes. Serve on cooked brown rice.

Yield: About 3 1/2 cups
Total Fat Grams: 3 to 4

CAJUN BLACKEYE PEAS

1/4 cup white wine or defatted stock
1 medium onion, chopped
2 ribs celery, sliced
2 cloves garlic, mashed
1/2 cup tomato sauce
1/4 cup honey
1/2 cup white wine
Salt and pepper to taste
1 to 5 splashes hot pepper sauce to taste
1 to 2 tsp. dry mustard
8 cups cooked blackeye peas

In a small skillet sauté the onion, celery and garlic in the 1/4 cup wine or stock until translucent. In a bowl, combine and mix thoroughly the tomato sauce, honey, 1/2 cup wine, salt pepper, hot sauce and mustard. Add the onion, celery and garlic. In a baking dish, toss together the peas and the sauce using care to avoid mashing the peas. Bake, uncovered, for 35 minutes in a 350° oven or until bubbling. Stir before serving.

Yield: About 10 cups
Total Fat Grams: 8

BLACKEYE PEAS AND POTATOES

I remember when I first moved to the South and was introduced to this bean which is a pea. I couldn't understand the love affair the southerner had with this legume. Try this recipe and you will fall in love, too!

Pam (5-second spray)
1 pound boiled potatoes
1 can (16 oz.) blackeye peas, drained
1 very large onion, sliced in 1/8 inch rounds
1 1/2 tsp. marjoram
1 1/2 Tbs. tomato paste mixed with 2 Tbs. water
Salt and pepper to taste

Boil the potatoes until a fork can pierce them. Drain, cool, slice into 1/4 inch rounds and set aside. Spray Pam in a large, non-stick frying pan. Sauté the onion in the Pam until translucent. Add the potatoes and fry 5 minutes. Add peas and continue to fry until heated through. If too dry, add some of the tomato paste mixture. Sprinkle with marjoram and add remaining tomato paste mixture. Toss the entire mixture until hot, seasoning to taste with salt and pepper.

Yield: 8 cups
Total Fat Grams: 4

REFRIED BEANS

If you're not in the mood to put this recipe together, or you don't have some of Jim's Beans ready to use, try one of the prepared numbers in a can. Rosarita's is wonderful, as is Old El Paso Vegetarian Refried Beans, both of which are made without lard, an ingredient often used in restaurant refried beans.

Olive Oil Pam
1 small onion, minced
1 tsp. garlic, minced
2 cups Jim's Beans (page 196)
1 fresh tomato, peeled and chopped

Spray Pam in non-stick pan and sauté onion and garlic until the onion is tender. Add the beans and tomato and cook for about 15 minutes. Mash or puree the mixture and serve with salsa.

Yield: About 2 cups
Total Fat Grams: 2

CREOLE RED BEANS AND RICE

1/4 cup white wine or defatted stock
2 green onions, thinly sliced
1 medium green bell pepper, minced
1 rib celery, minced
1/2 tsp. garlic powder
2 tsp. granulated chicken or beef bouillon
1/2 tsp. dried thyme
1/4 tsp. cayenne pepper
1 can (16 oz.) red kidney beans with liquid
1 cup uncooked Uncle Ben's Converted Long Grain Rice
1/2 cup tomato sauce
1 1/4 cups boiling water

Sauté the green onions, green pepper and celery in the wine or stock for about 4 or 5 minutes. Add the garlic, thyme and cayenne. Stir together for about 15 seconds. Add kidney beans and liquid, rice, tomato sauce and water. Mix all ingredients and simmer, covered for 20 minutes or until liquid has been absorbed and rice is tender.

Yield: About 5 cups
Total Fat Grams: 3

THE BEST BLACK BEANS

We tried this recipe with olive oil as it originally appeared on a can of black beans, back in the days before we knew better. The taste has not suffered one iota. As a small serving this can be a side vegetable or an appetizer. We like it as a meal.

1/2 cup white wine, divided
1 medium onion, chopped
8 ounces pimento, drained and sliced
2 cans (16 oz. ea.) black beans, partially drained
1/2 tsp. oregano leaves, crushed
1/2 tsp. sugar
Salt and hot pepper sauce to taste
Steamed rice

Sauté the onion in 1/4 cup white wine. Add the pimento when onion is soft and cook through for about 2 minutes. Add the beans, the additional 1/4 cup wine, oregano and sugar. Simmer until somewhat creamy looking, about 25 minutes. Serve over steamed rice. Add salt and hot pepper sauce to taste

Yield: About 5 cups
Total Fat Grams: 5

BLACK BEANS WITH RICE

1/4 cup white wine or defatted stock
1 medium onion, chopped
1 green bell pepper, minced
1 rib celery, minced
1/2 tsp. garlic powder
2 cups water
1/2 tsp. thyme
1 cup Uncle Ben's Converted Rice, uncooked
2 cans (16 oz. ea.) black beans, drained
1/4 cup fresh parsley, chopped
Pepper or hot pepper sauce to taste

Sauté the onion, pepper and celery in the wine or stock until soft. Add the garlic and thyme, rice and water. Bring to a boil, reduce heat and simmer, covered, for 10 minutes. Add the beans, cover, simmer 5 minutes. Add parsley, cover and simmer 5 minutes more, or until water is absorbed. Add pepper or hot pepper sauce to taste.

Yield: About 6 cups
Total Fat Grams: 5

LENA'S LENTIL BAKE

3/4 cup lentils, uncooked, rinsed
2 2/3 cups water
1/2 cup brown rice, uncooked
1 medium onion, chopped
1 1/4 cups white wine
1/2 tsp. dried basil
1/2 tsp. oregano leaves
1/4 tsp. thyme leaves
1/2 tsp. garlic powder
2 oz. Healthy Choice Pasteurized Processed Cheese Product, in 1/2 inch pieces

Combine all ingredients, except the cheese. Place in oven-proof casserole dish and bake, uncovered, for 1 1/2 to 2 hours at 350°. This casserole should be moist but not runny. Sprinkle the pieces of cheese on top and bake for 5 minutes.

Yield: About 4 cups
Total Fat Grams: 0

LENTILS AND RICE

1/4 cup white wine or defatted stock
1 large onion, chopped
1 carrot, chopped
1/2 tsp. thyme leaves
1/2 tsp. marjoram
2 cups defatted chicken stock or broth
1 cup water
1 cup lentils, uncooked, rinsed
2 cans (8 oz. ea.) tomato sauce
1 cup white wine
1/4 cup fresh parsley, chopped
Cooked brown rice

Sauté the onion and carrot in the wine for about 4 minutes. Add the thyme and marjoram and sauté for 1 more minute. Add the rest of the ingredients, except the rice, and simmer for 1 hour. Serve over the hot cooked rice.

Yield: About 5 cups
Total Fat Grams: 3

SWEET LENTILS

1 cup lentils, uncooked, rinsed
3 cups water
2 Tbs. brown sugar
2 Tbs. white wine vinegar
Freshly ground black pepper to taste

Bring lentils and water to a boil. Cover and simmer, gently, for 30 minutes, until lentils are tender. Check pot every now and then to see if more water is needed. While the lentils are cooking, simmer sugar and vinegar just until the sugar is dissolved. When the lentils are tender, stir in sugar-vinegar mixture and simmer for 5 minutes. Season to taste with pepper.

Yield: About 3 cups
Total Fat Grams: 1

LENTILS, SPINACH AND RICE

1/4 cup white wine or defatted stock
1 large onion, chopped
1 rib celery, sliced diagonally
2 cloves garlic, mashed
Olive Oil Pam
1 cup lentils, uncooked, rinsed
4 cups defatted chicken stock or broth
1/2 cup white rice, uncooked
2 packages (10 oz. ea. package) frozen spinach, thawed
1/2 cup additional stock
Salt and pepper to taste

Sauté the onion, celery and garlic in the wine or stock, until translucent. Add the lentils, spray with the Olive Oil Pam, and mix the vegetables and lentils to enhance the flavor with a hint of the olive oil. Set aside. Bring the 4 cups stock to a boil, add to the vegetable-lentil mixture and return to boiling. Reduce the heat to low and simmer, covered, for 20 minutes or until the lentils are just tender. Add rice, stir and bring to a boil. Reduce heat and simmer 15 minutes. Add the spinach and additional 1/2 cup stock. Cover and cook until the rice is done. Season with salt and pepper to taste.

Yield: About 6 cups
Total Fat Grams: 4

CURRIED RICE

1 1/2 cups brown rice, uncooked
3 cups water
1 medium onion, chopped
1 clove garlic, minced
1/2 medium green bell pepper, chopped
1/4 cup white wine or defatted stock
1/2 cup raisins
1/4 tsp. curry powder or more to taste
1 cup water

Boil 3 cups water and stir in the rice. Cook, covered, for 45 minutes. In a separate pot, sauté the onion, garlic and pepper in the wine or stock to soften. Add raisins, curry powder and additional 1 cup water. Simmer 10 minutes. Combine with the rice and cook together for 15 minutes.

Yield: About 5 cups
Total Fat Grams: Less than 1

GREEN RICE

1 cup white rice, uncooked
1/2 small onion, chopped
1 Tbs. dried basil
1 1/2 tsp. granulated chicken bouillon
2 cups boiling water

Add all ingredients to the boiling water and cook on low heat, covered, for 20 minutes.

Yield: 2 cups
Total Fat Grams: Less than 1

HAWAIIAN RICE

This dish is best prepared in a wok.

1/4 pound mushrooms, sliced
1 small green bell pepper, diced
1 small red bell pepper, diced
1 medium onion, chopped
1 can (8 oz.) pineapple chunks in natural juice
2 tsp. dried leaf basil or 2 Tbs. fresh basil
1/4 tsp. ground ginger
1/2 cup water chestnuts, diced
2 cups cooked rice, cold
Salt and pepper to taste

Place wok over high heat. Spray with Pam. When the wok is hot, add the mushrooms, bell peppers and onion. Stir-fry 1 minute. Sprinkle about 2 Tbs. pineapple juice over the hot vegetables and discard the rest of the juice. Cover and steam until the mushrooms start softening. Increase heat to high, add all ingredients, except the rice, and stir-fry for 1/2 minute. Stir in the rice and stir-fry until all ingredients are hot. Season to taste with salt and pepper.

Yield: About 5 cups
Total Fat Grams: 1

FAUX FRIED RICE

2 cups Uncle Ben's Converted Rice, uncooked
4 cups boiling water
1 rib celery, thinly sliced
1 medium onion, thinly sliced
1 1/2 Tbs. granulated chicken or beef bouillon
1/2 cup mushrooms, sliced
Soy sauce to taste
Egg Beaters (optional)

Combine all ingredients except Egg Beaters. Bring water back up to boil. Reduce heat and simmer, covered for 20 minutes. Additional vegetables such as water chestnuts, bamboo shoots, bean sprouts and frozen peas may be thrown in the pot along with the onions and mushrooms to enhance the flavor. Add a few dashes of soy sauce to taste or pass soy sauce at the table. You may scramble the equivalent of one egg to thinly slice and place on top of the rice as a garnish.

Yield: About 5 cups
Total Fat Grams: Less than 1

RED RICE

Red rice is a natural for the freezer, stored in meal size packages. Thawed and heated in the microwave, it tastes as good as just-made. It's great with Jim's Beans, Quickie Chili Beans, Vegetarian Chili or Best Black Beans. You can eat it on the side as a vegetable, or add sliced turkey or chicken with the onion and pepper to make a meal in one pot. Thinly sliced celery, carrots or frozen peas or lima beans may be other add-ons to this versatile dish.

1 large can (15 oz.) tomato sauce
6-1/2 cups boiling water(approx.)
4 cups Uncle Ben's Converted Rice, uncooked
1 large onion, chopped
1 medium green bell pepper, chopped
2 Tbs. granulated chicken, vegetable or beef bouillon

Place tomato sauce in a measuring cup and add enough of the boiling water to make up 8 cups. Combine all ingredients. Bring water back up to boil. Reduce heat and simmer, covered for 20 minutes or until all liquid is absorbed. Toss with fork to fluff up the rice.

Yield: 8 cups
Total Fat Grams: 1

BROCCOLI RICE

This casserole was the way I got my kids to eat broccoli when they were small and it's still a family favorite.

2 cups Uncle Ben's Converted Rice, uncooked
1 large onion, sliced thin
2 cans Campbell's Healthy Request Cream of Mushroom soup, undiluted
4 cups boiling water
3 Tbs. vegetable, chicken or beef bouillon granules
6 cups broccoli flowerets fresh, or frozen and defrosted
2 Tbs. Worcestershire sauce
4 oz. Healthy Choice Pasteurized Process Cheese Product or fat free grated cheddar

Saucepan: Combine all ingredients, except the cheese. Bring to boil. Cover and simmer for 20 minutes or until all liquid is absorbed and the rice is cooked. Then add the cheese, mix through and cover for 5 minutes. The cheese will melt and the dish is ready to serve.
Oven: Combine all ingredients, except cheese, as above. Bake at 350° for 1 hour, covered. Add cheese, mix through, and sprinkle some grated cheddar on top. Bake, uncovered, for 10 minutes.

Yield: 6 cups
Total Fat Grams: 11

MARINARA SAUCE

This is the base sauce for any of the many variations you will see throughout these pages. It may be used in any other recipes you find in other publications calling for a marinara sauce and will appear later in this book in both the seafood and chicken sections. As you can see, there's an abundance of sauce here...it freezes so well, and can be used in so many recipes, that we always prepare the base recipe for freezing. When unexpected company arrives, thaw out this sauce, add clams, shrimp or chicken and you're a culinary genius!

If you prefer a thicker sauce simmer the sauce longer to evaporate the liquid. However, if a thinner sauce is your preference, add water during the last hour or so of simmering to achieve the desired consistency.

1/4 cup white wine or defatted stock
1 large onion, chopped
1 Tbs. garlic, minced
2 Tbs. mixed dried Italian Seasonings
1 Tbs. oregano leaves
2 tsp. thyme leaves
2 Tbs. granulated beef or chicken bouillon
2 tsp. crushed red pepper flakes, optional
3 cans (16 oz. ea.) Italian plum tomatoes with juice
2 bay leaves
2 cans (6 oz. ea.) tomato paste
1 cup water
2 cans (15 oz. ea.) tomato sauce or puree
2 tsp. sugar, white or brown

Sauté the onion and garlic in the wine or stock with the seasonings and bouillon granules until the onions are soft. Add the tomatoes and break up with a spoon. Add the bay leaves and simmer on medium, uncovered, for 20 minutes. Add the tomato paste and sauce with the sugar and simmer on low heat, partially covered, for 3 to 4 hours. If puree is used, the sauce will be thicker and may require additional water. Individual taste prevails. Remove from heat and allow to cool. Refrigerate overnight or for at least 6 hours for flavors to set up and sauce to thicken.

Yield: 10 to 12 cups
Total Fat Grams: Less than 1

MUSHROOM MARINARA SAUCE

4 cups Marinara Sauce (page 226)
1 cup mushrooms, sliced

Heat Marinara Sauce in large saucepan. Add the mushrooms and cook on medium heat until mushrooms are soft. May be used in any recipes calling for the basic Marinara Sauce.

Yield: 4 cups
Total Fat Grams: 0

SPINACH LASAGNA ROLL-UPS

This is the recipe for lasagna that I talk about earlier in the book. We had prepared this with ground beef at first. Then we switched to ground turkey. Now we know it's a crowd pleaser as it appears here.

8 lasagna noodles, cooked according to pkg. directions
1 box frozen spinach, cooked and squeezed dry
8 oz. fat-free cottage cheese
Basic Marinara Sauce (page 226)

Spread the noodles out on a table. Place an even amount of cottage cheese and spinach on each of 8 noodles, roll and place, seam side down, in a pan in which a layer of sauce has been spread. Pour about 1 cup sauce over the roll-ups and bake at 350° for 50 minutes.

Yield: 8 roll-ups
Total Fat Grams: 5

KIM'S SPINACH LASAGNA

16 to 18 lasagna noodles, cooked
Basic Marinara Sauce (page 226)
8 oz. fat-free cottage cheese or fat-free ricotta
1 box frozen spinach, cooked and squeezed dry
Fat-free mozzarella, shredded

Cook and drain the noodles and set aside. Layer the marinara sauce in the bottom of a 9 x 12 rectangular baking pan. Mix together the cottage cheese and spinach and layer 1/2 the mixture on the noodles, spreading the mixture evenly. Follow with a layer of Marinara, then noodles. Repeat with mixture, Marinara and noodles, finishing with the sauce. Sprinkle the shredded fat-free mozzarella on top and bake at 350° for 30—45 minutes or until heated through and bubbling.

Yield: 9 x 12 lasagna
Total Fat Grams: 7

SIMPLE SPINACH LENTIL LASAGNA

This wonderful lasagna will knock your socks off! It's the easiest lasagna to make...ever! The noodles are NOT pre-cooked! That's right. You layer in the lasagna noodles, raw, and they cook in the sauce in the oven! This lasagna is no tougher to prepare than playing cards. The most difficult part of making lasagna has always been layering the sticky noodles. We can thank our dear friend, Lou Cimaglia, who really knows how to cook "Italian," for this ingenious labor-saver. The lentils lend the crunch of pine nuts to your mouth as you chew. What a dish!

5 cups Basic Marinara Sauce (page 226), divided
1 lb. uncooked lasagna noodles, divided
2 packages (15 oz. ea.) fat-free ricotta cheese
1/2 cup fat-free egg substitute
2 boxes frozen leaf spinach, thawed and squeezed dry
1 8 oz. package shredded fat-free mozzarella cheese
1 Tbs. dried Italian seasoning
1/8 tsp. ground thyme or 1/4 tsp. dried thyme leaves
3 Tbs. lentils, uncooked

Cut the leaf spinach to about 1 inch pieces and tear apart. Combine with ricotta cheese, egg substitute, along with 4 Tbs. mozzarella cheese, Italian seasoning and thyme. Spray a lasagna pan (7" x 11" x 2 1/2") with Pam or Mazola Oil Spray. Cover the bottom of the pan with 1 cup Marinara sauce. Lay in 3 to 4 noodles in their dry state. Follow with 1/3 spinach/ricotta mixture. Sprinkle 1 Tbs. lentils evenly over the mixture and then cover with 1 cup Marinara. Sprinkle with about 1/4 of the shredded cheese remaining in the package. Repeat procedure with 2 more layers of noodles, spinach/ricotta mixture, lentils, 1 cup Marinara and shredded cheese, as above. Lay in noodles, remaining Marinara and remaining shredded mozzarella. Cover tightly with aluminum foil. Bake at 350° for 1 hour, uncover and bake for another 10 minutes. This dish can be served immediately, however, it's even better after a day in the refrigerator to "set up." It's great baked to reheat at 350° or microwave until heated through. After firming in the fridge, you can cut into serving sizes and freeze for future dinners.

Yield: 9 x 12 lasagna
Total Fat Grams: 7

ZUCCHINI SPINACH LASAGNA

9 to 12 lasagna noodles, cooked
1/4 cup white wine or defatted stock
1 cup onion, chopped
1/2 cup green bell pepper. chopped
2 medium zucchini, sliced
4 cups Basic Marinara Sauce (page 226)
1 tsp. salt
1/4 tsp. dried basil
1/4 tsp. dried oregano
1 package (10 oz.) frozen spinach, thawed and drained
2 pounds fat-free cottage cheese, drained
8 oz. grated fat-free mozzarella

Cook and drain the noodles and set aside. Sauté the onion and green pepper in the wine or stock until tender. Add the remaining ingredients except the lasagna noodles, spinach, cottage cheese and the mozzarella. Simmer slowly for 20 minutes. Place a thin layer of this mixture in the bottom of a 9 x 12 non-stick baking pan. Layer in the lasagna noodles, sauce mixture, spinach and cottage cheese. Sprinkle on the mozzarella. Repeat layers, ending with mozzarella and a thin layer of sauce. Bake at 350° for about 35 to 40 minutes or until heated through.

Yield: 9 x 12 lasagna
Total Fat Grams: 7

PASTA FAGIOLE

2 Tbs. white wine or defatted stock
1 small onion, diced
1/2 carrot, diced
1/2 rib celery, minced
1 clove garlic, minced
1 can (8 oz.) tomato sauce or 1 cup chopped tomatoes
1/2 tsp. dried oregano
2 Tbs. fresh basil, chopped or 1 tsp. dried basil
1 can (16 oz.) cannellini beans, drained and rinsed
1 cup dried elbow macaroni, uncooked
Freshly ground black pepper

Sauté the onion, carrot, celery and garlic in the wine or stock until vegetables are very soft. If necessary, add more liquid, cover and simmer. Add the tomato sauce, oregano and basil and simmer 5 minutes. Add the beans and simmer another 10 minutes. Mash about half the beans against the side of the pot. Add dry pasta and simmer for about 10 minutes more or until the pasta is cooked. Season with pepper.

Yield: About 5 to 6 cups
Total Fat Grams: 3

NOODLE/PEA CASSEROLE

1/2 pound ribbon noodles (eggless)
1 can Healthy Request Cream of Mushroom Soup (undiluted)
1 1/2 tsp. granulated chicken bouillon
1/4 cup water
1/2 tsp. garlic powder
1/2 onion, thinly sliced
3/4 cup frozen peas
3/4 cup mushrooms, thickly sliced
1/2 cup Healthy Choice Grated Cheddar Cheese

Cook noodles according to package directions, rinse, drain and place in a casserole dish with the Cream of Mushroom soup. Sauté the onion in the bouillon, garlic and water until tender. Add the peas and mushrooms to the onion mixture and cook on low heat until the peas are thawed. Add to the remaining ingredients and mix well. Bake at 350° until heated through, about 20 minutes. Sprinkle the cheese on top, replace for 10 minutes for a golden, crusty top.

Yield: About 5 cups
Total Fat Grams: 8

PASTA IN BROTH

1/2 cup dry white wine
1 onion, sliced
1 green bell pepper, sliced
1 tsp. garlic, minced
1/2 pound mushrooms, sliced
1 tsp. dried oregano
2 Tbs. fresh parsley
1/2 cup defatted stock
2 to 3 cups cooked vermicelli

Poach all vegetables and herbs in the wine until soft. Add stock and simmer until cooked down by one-quarter. Toss pasta in pot with sauce to heat through.

Yield: About 5 cups
Total Fat Grams: 6—8

PASTA PRIMAVERA

12 oz. spaghetti, uncooked
2 Tbs. white wine or defatted stock
1 1/2 cups mushrooms, sliced
1 onion, thinly sliced
2 cloves garlic, minced
2 cups broccoli flowerets
2 cups zucchini, halved and sliced
1 cup carrots, thinly sliced
1/3 cup dry white wine
1/4 cup fresh parsley, chopped
2 tsp. dried basil
1/4 tsp. salt
1/8 tsp. pepper
6 Tbs. fat free Parmesan cheese

Cook the spaghetti al dente, according to package directions. Drain well in a colander and set aside. In a large pan, or wok, sauté the mushrooms, onion and garlic in 2 Tbs. white wine or stock for 1 to 2 minutes. Add the broccoli, zucchini and carrots and cook, stirring, 2 to 3 minutes more. Add the wine, parsley, basil, salt and pepper. Simmer 5 minutes or until the vegetables are crisp-tender. Run hot water over the spaghetti in the colander, drain and add to the vegetables with the cheese. Toss & serve.

Yield: About 10 to 12 cups
Total Fat Grams: 5

PASTA WITH SHITAKE MUSHROOMS

8 Shitake mushrooms
1/2 pound pasta, cooked and drained
1/4 cup wine
1 clove garlic, minced
1/2 medium onion, thinly sliced
5 plum tomatoes, chopped (if canned, reserve the juice)
3/4 tsp. dried oregano
1/2 cup fresh parsley, chopped
1 Tbs. plus 1 tsp. granulated beef or chicken bouillon
1 cup water
Crushed hot red pepper to taste
Salt and pepper to taste

Soak the mushrooms until soft, about 20 minutes. Remove the stems and thinly slice. Set aside. Prepare the pasta, drain and set aside. Sauté the garlic and onion in the wine until soft. Add all other ingredients except the pasta and simmer, stirring often, about 15 to 20 minutes. Add additional water, wine or tomato juice from the canned tomatoes, as necessary. Add the pasta and toss well. Season to taste.

Yield: About 8 cups
Total Fat Grams: 4

PASTA WITH SPINACH

1 cup chicken stock
1 packet prepared Butter Buds
8 ounces fresh spinach, about 6 cups
1 tsp. garlic powder
1 tsp. celery seed
1 tsp. dried oregano
Crushed red pepper (optional)
1 Tbs. cornstarch dissolved in 1 Tbs. cold water
4 cups very thin spaghetti, cooked
Fat-free Parmesan cheese to taste

Bring the Butter Buds and stock to the boil. Add the spinach, garlic, celery seed (and the red pepper, if you like it hot), and wilt the spinach. Immediately add the cornstarch and as soon as the sauce is thickened, pour over the pasta. If you've heated the pasta under hot running water, you may toss the spaghetti right in the pot to reheat with the sauce. Sprinkle with the Parmesan cheese and serve.

Yield: 4 cups
Total Fat Grams: 2

VEGETABLE LO MEIN

8 oz. cooked vermicelli
1 cup defatted stock
2 tsp. light soy sauce
4 tsp. heavy soy sauce
2 tsp. sugar
2 tsp. diced fresh ginger
2 tsp. sherry
4 tsp. cornstarch
1/4 cup white wine or defatted stock
2 cloves garlic, minced
1 medium onion, thickly sliced
2 cups broccoli flowerets
2 cups cauliflower flowerets
1 tsp. sesame oil

Place the vermicelli in a colander and set aside. Combine 1 cup stock, soy sauces, sugar, ginger, sherry and cornstarch. Set aside. Heat 1/4 cup white wine or stock in the wok and add garlic, onion, broccoli and cauliflower. Stir fry until crisp-tender. Add the liquid mixture and stir-fry until sauce thickens. Remove from the heat and cover to keep warm. Run hot water over the vermicelli and drain well. Place in a large bowl and toss with the sesame oil. Place the vermicelli in the wok with the vegetables and if necessary turn heat on high and toss just to reheat. Serve immediately.

Yield: About 9 to 10 cups
Total Fat Grams: 9

VEGETABLES

Most of our social world has considered the vegetable serving as a side dish or garnish to help enhance the main attraction...the meat. We have a different approach to the vegetable, whereby the meat becomes the condiment and the veggie becomes the king of the hill.

As you become more familiar with this lifestyle, you'll find more and more of these dishes that you will look forward to for a filling and satisfying meal. Some actually are mealmakers and some you will serve as side dishes. You will wonder whatever happened to those bland, tinny-tasting green beans or the soggy spinach that came out of a can that were, at one time, the "necessary" accompaniment to the meat on the plate.

Stir-frying adds a whole new dimension to the preparation of vegetables. At one time a staple utensil found only in the Oriental kitchen, the wok has taken a revered place of honor in American cookery. One of the most versatile of pans, the wok allows for steaming, stir-frying, stewing, poaching and toss-cooking. If you don't already own a wok, I recommend the purchase of a heavy duty wok. After using it just a few times you will wonder how you ever got along in your kitchen without one. Remember how you felt after one week having had your microwave in action? Your reaction to giving up your wok will be similar to the panic you would feel with thoughts of living without your microwave.

Woks come in a variety of sizes and metals. The 14-inch wok is most often recommended for the average American kitchen since it will handle the most common quantities for small meals or company cooking. You may buy one and find a second wok in another size would come in handy and end up in a two-wok kitchen. Use your common sense when choosing the size of your first wok. Try to find the thick and heavy spun steel. This wok will retain the highest and most even heat. Copper will cause spotty, uneven heating, while the stainless steel conducts heat more slowly and may result in sticking or burning. Electric woks produce an unevenly heated surface and do not perform as well as the authentic Oriental spun steel wok. You may find a wok with a non-stick finish that is heavy enough to stir-fry properly and offers the advantage of the non-stick cooking. In fact, I found a 12-inch wok with a non-stick finish that has revolutionized cooking in my kitchen. When I want to prepare soup or a large pot of sauce for freezing, such as a Marinara, I use a saucepan or deep cooker. Otherwise, I pull out this wok because it is the easiest utensil I've ever cooked with. Once you become accustomed to the feel of the handle and the balanced weight of the wok, you'll see what I mean. For larger stir-frys I use my authentic, seasoned wok.

Seasoning the wok is essential before using and is well worth the effort since this wok can last you a lifetime if it is seasoned properly to begin with and then maintained correctly. Season your new wok as directed in the material which accompanies your new purchase or follow these simple instructions: if the wok has a coating on it which feels greasy or gummy, sprinkle lighter fluid on the surface before scrubbing; scrub with soap and hot water. Introduce about a teaspoon of peanut oil to the interior surface and rub in well.

Use a paper towel and rub until the towel remains clean. Wash the wok with a soft nylon pad in hot water. Dry the wok over medium heat for several minutes, rinse with hot water, rub again with oil and then dry over medium heat again. Repeat this procedure one or two times and you will notice the wok has turned darker and may be discolored.

Keep the wok clean in the manner described above, with a soft nylon pad and hot water, drying well after cleaning and applying oil from time to time. The wok will continue to darken and mellow with age and as it becomes older it will cook even better.

When stir-frying or toss-cooking, use an Oriental-style spatula with curved sides. This spatula will fit the curved bottom of your wok better than the flat version you already have in your kitchen. I found a wooden spatula that does beautifully with my non-stick wok and use the Oriental-style spatula, which is steel, with my steel wok. Learn to deftly handle a pair of chopsticks and expose yourself to some of the wonders of Oriental cooking. You'll find some of these recipes interspersed with the potatoes, cabbages, green beans and squash.

Whether you opt for the Oriental flavoring or go for the more American and Continental style preparation, your appreciation of the vegetable and its place at your table is about to be enhanced. By adding and adjusting the spices and condiments in any of the vegetable dishes that follow on these next pages, you may alter the flavors to better suit your own taste.

Try some of the one-dish meals or make a meal of a combination of different veggies and see if you really miss the meat. You may be in for a surprise. Do experiment to broaden your experience with the noble vegetable.

RATATOUILLE

You'll notice the use of Balsamic vinegar in this recipe. If you haven't yet, become familiar with some of the more exotic vinegars and you'll find some aromatic and delicate flavorings you'll learn to enjoy along with the old standby white and wine.

1 medium onion, chopped
2 tsp. defatted stock
1 small eggplant, cubed
2 small zucchini, cubed
3 medium tomatoes, chopped
1 green bell pepper, chopped
1/4 cup fresh parsley, minced
2 cloves garlic, minced
2 shallots, minced
3 Tbs. tomato paste
1 tsp. dried basil
1 tsp. dried thyme
1 Tbs. balsamic vinegar

Combine the onion and stock in a 2 quart casserole dish, cover, and microwave on high about 1 1/2 minutes or until the onion is tender. Add all ingredients except the vinegar, stir well, cover, and microwave for about 15 to 17 minutes, stirring occasionally until vegetables are tender. Stir in vinegar and let stand 10 minutes. Serve with hot French bread.

Yield: About 6 to 8 cups
Total Fat Grams: Less than 1

SQUASH AND ONION CHEESE BAKE

Covering the pot after adding the cheese, and steaming the contents until the cheese melts, will work in place of the oven. Rotel is found in the canned tomato section of your store and is a combination of tomatoes and jalapeño peppers. It adds a kick to this dish. You may remember seeing Rotel used in the Chili Con Queso recipe in the Hors D'Oeuvres section of the book.

6 zucchini, cut in 1/2 inch slices
3 yellow squash, cut in 1/2 inch slices
1 large onion, thickly sliced
1 to 2 Tbs. dried mixed Italian seasonings
1 Tbs. granulated beef or chicken bouillon
1 can (15 oz.) tomatoes, drained and chopped or 1 can Rotel (if you like it hot)
2 oz. Healthy Choice Pasteurized Process Cheese Product, broken into chunks

Combine all ingredients except cheese, and cook, uncovered, on low heat until onions are cooked through, about 30 minutes. Place the cheese on top and bake at 350° or until the cheese melts.

Yield: About 6 cups
Total Fat Grams: 1

SQUASH ORIENTAL

1/4 cup defatted stock
2 cups zucchini, sliced
2 cups cabbage, shredded
1 cup fresh spinach, chopped
1 cup fresh bean sprouts
1 can water chestnuts, sliced
Soy sauce to taste

Heat the stock in a wok, add vegetables and stir-fry until crisp-tender. Add more stock, if necessary, to avoid sticking. Do not overcook or the veggies will be soggy. Season with sauce soy to taste.

Yield: About 6 cups
Total Fat Grams: Less than 1

ZUCCHINI WITH CABBAGE & BEETS

2 Tbs. white wine or defatted stock
1 onion, minced
1 clove garlic, minced
2 fresh beets, sliced
1 green bell pepper, chopped
2 medium zucchini, sliced
2 cups cabbage, shredded
1 tomato, peeled and seeded, chopped in chunks
1 tsp. dried rosemary
1 tsp. dried thyme
1/2 cup water or defatted stock

Sauté the onion and garlic in the wine or stock until tender. Add the remaining ingredients and simmer, covered, for about 20 minutes, or until the vegetables are tender. Season to taste.

Yield: About 6 cups
Total Fat Grams: Less than 1

ZUCCHINI AND TOMATOES

6 small zucchini, sliced 1/4-inch thick
1/2 onion, thinly sliced
1 medium green pepper, thinly sliced
2 tomatoes, peeled and thinly sliced
Olive Oil Pam
2 Tbs. fresh parsley, chopped
3 Tbs. grated fat free Parmesan cheese, optional

Steam the zucchini and set aside. Then steam the onion and set aside, separately, and repeat with the bell pepper. Treat a shallow casserole or baking pan with Olive Oil Pam, about a 5 second spray. Layer the vegetables in the pan starting with the zucchini first and then alternating with the onion and green pepper, ending with the tomatoes. Sprinkle the parsley on top. Finish off with the Parmesan cheese, if desired. Cover and bake at 350° for about 15 minutes or until heated through.

Yield: 3 to 4 cups
Total Fat Grams: 3

STIR-FRIED ZUCCHINI AND GREEN BEANS

1/4 cup white wine or defatted stock
1 pound fresh green beans, cut in 2 inch pieces
3 cups sliced zucchini
1 rib celery, thinly sliced
1 Tbs. lemon juice
Soy sauce
2 to 3 Tbs. defatted stock or broth
1 tsp. cornstarch

Stir-fry beans in 1/4 cup wine or stock for about 2 minutes. Add zucchini, celery, lemon juice and a splash of soy sauce. Stir fry for about 2 to 3 minutes until crisp-tender. Add the 2 Tbs. stock or broth and corn starch which has been dissolved in a Tbs. of broth. Cook on high until vegetables are glazed and the sauce is thickened.

Yield: About 6 cups
Total Fat Grams: 1

MEXI-SQUASH

1/2 cup white wine or defatted stock
2 zucchini, sliced
2 yellow squash, sliced
1 medium onion, sliced
1 tomato, peeled and chopped
1 1/2 cups whole kernel corn
2 green bell peppers, thinly sliced
Salt, pepper and hot pepper sauce to taste

Place all ingredients in the pot, except seasonings, and cook on medium heat until vegetables are tender. Season to taste. Really good served on Red Rice.

Yield: About 4 cups
Total Fat Grams: 2

ZUCCHINI-VEGGIE MEDLEY

1/4 cup white wine or defatted stock
1 medium onion, chopped
1 clove garlic, minced
1 cup celery, chopped
2 cups zucchini, chopped
1 cup carrot, chopped
1 cup peas
1 cup lima beans, cooked
1 red bell pepper, chopped
1/2 to 1 cup defatted stock or broth

Sauté the onion, garlic and celery in the 1/4 cup wine or stock. Add all other ingredients. Determine amount of stock or broth to suit your own taste. Simmer, uncovered, about 15 minutes or until vegetables are tender. Season to taste.

Yield: About 6 cups
Total Fat Grams: 2

SQUASH AND PASTA

1 pound pasta
Olive Oil Pam
1 onion, thinly sliced
1 clove garlic, minced
1 medium zucchini, julienned
1 medium yellow squash, julienned
1 Tbs. mixed dried Italian seasonings
3 Tbs. white wine or defatted stock
Fresh ground pepper
Fat free Parmesan cheese (optional)

Cook the pasta according to package directions, drain in a colander and set aside. Spray the Pam in a large pan (2 1/2 second spray) and sauté onion and garlic until just tender. You may want to add a splash of stock or wine if the pan gets too dry. Add all the other ingredients, except the cheese, and cook on medium-high heat until all the vegetables are crisp-tender. Run pasta under hot water to heat, and drain well. Toss pasta with a 2 1/2 second spray of Olive Oil Pam. Place the vegetable mixture on top of the pasta. Sprinkle each dish with 1 Tbs. Parmesan cheese, if desired.

Yield: About 12 to 14 cups
Total Fat Grams: 10

ZUCCHINI CHEESE BAKE

1/4 cup white wine or defatted stock
2 medium zucchini, sliced
1 onion, thinly sliced
1 can (15 oz.) stewed tomatoes
1/2 pound fat-free cottage cheese
1/2 tsp. dried basil
4 Tbs. fat free Parmesan cheese

Sauté the onion and zucchini in the wine or stock until crisp-tender. Partially drain the tomatoes. Puree the cottage cheese and basil in a blender or food processor. Prepare a casserole with a light spray of Pam or other non-stick spray. Alternate layers of cottage cheese, zucchini mixture and tomatoes. Sprinkle Parmesan cheese on top. Bake at 350° for 20—25 minutes.

Yield: 4 to 5 cups
Total Fat Grams: 2

PEPPERS AND TOMATOES

2 red bell peppers, sliced in rings
2 green bell peppers, sliced in rings
1/2 cup defatted stock
4 onions, cut in wedges
6 tomatoes, cored and cut in wedges
Salt & pepper to taste

Sauté the peppers and onions in the stock for about 10 minutes on a medium heat, stirring often. Add tomatoes and cook 10 minutes longer. Season to taste.

Yield: 8 to 10 cups
Total Fat Grams: Less than 1

GLAZED CARROTS WITH SPICES

3/4 cup water
8 medium carrots, sliced on the diagonal, 1/2 inch thick
1 cinnamon stick
2 tsp. honey
3/4 tsp. ground cumin
1/2 tsp. ground ginger
1/4 tsp. ground coriander
1/8 tsp. cayenne pepper
2 tsp. honey
2 tsp. lemon juice

Boil the water in a large pan. When boiling, add the carrots and dry seasonings. Reduce heat to a low rolling boil and simmer, covered, for 15 minutes. Uncover, add the honey and lemon juice. Return to high heat and boil until the water has evaporated and carrots are tender, about 4 to 5 minutes.

Yield: About 6 cups
Total Fat Grams: 1

STIR-FRIED GREEN BEANS

1/4 cup white wine or defatted stock
1 clove garlic, minced
2 to 3 cups fresh green beans, cut in 1 inch pieces
1/2 cup defatted chicken stock or broth
1 tsp. soy sauce
1/2 tsp. sugar
1 tsp. cornstarch
1 Tbs. cold water

Heat the wine or stock in a wok and add the garlic with a pinch of salt. Sauté for about 1 minute and add the green beans. Stir-fry the beans for 3 minutes and add the broth, soy sauce and sugar. Cover and steam over moderate heat for 3 to 4 minutes or until the beans are crisp-tender. Dissolve the cornstarch in the cold water and stir into the beans until the sauce is thickened. Serve on steamed rice. If you like it spicy hot, check out the following recipe for Szechuan String Beans.

Yield: 2 to 3 cups
Total Fat Grams: 1

SZECHUAN STRING BEANS

This recipe is as close to the preceding Stir-Fried Green Beans as a fraternal twin. There are just a few changes to give this dish the added zip of Szechuan cuisine for those who like it hot. If you can't find the stir-fry sauce I list here, check at your own Oriental food market or your supermarket in the Oriental food section and check the fat grams on the label to see how much oil the product has included in the ingredients. If you just add the crushed red pepper, that alone will give you the Szechuan heat without the added oil.

1/4 cup white wine or defatted stock
1 clove garlic, minced
2 to 3 cups fresh green beans, cut in half
1/4 cup defatted chicken stock or broth
2 Tbs. Rice Road Stir-Fry Sauce Fresh Garlic & Ginger
1 tsp. soy sauce
1/4 tsp. sugar
1 tsp. cornstarch
1 Tbs. cold water
Crushed red pepper to taste

Prepare as in Stir-Fried Green Beans. Add the crushed red pepper to taste to add more heat. Serve on steamed rice.

Yield: 2 to 3 cups
Total Fat Grams: 7

GREEN BEANS WITH MUSHROOMS

This is a side dish veggie rather than a meal. If you'd like to stretch this into a dinner dish, add 1/2 cup defatted stock, 1 Tbs. cornstarch dissolved in 1 to 2 Tbs. cold water and to bring out some interest in the sauce, add some basil and Italian seasonings. Heat until the sauce thickens and serve with pasta.

1/4 cup white wine or defatted stock
1 medium onion, thinly sliced
1 clove garlic, minced
1 pound green beans
1/2 pound mushrooms, thickly sliced
Salt and freshly ground pepper

Sauté the onion and garlic in the wine or stock until crisp-tender. Add the green beans and cook on medium heat for 3 to 5 minutes. Add the mushrooms and cook on medium heat until the mushrooms are soft. If necessary add more stock to avoid sticking. Season to taste.

Yield: 4 to 5 cups
Total Fat Grams: Less than 1

LIMA BEANS AND TOMATOES

2 boxes (10 oz. ea.) frozen lima beans
2 cups tomatoes, chopped or 2 cups stewed tomatoes with 1/4 cup juice
1/2 cup celery, diced
1/2 cup green bell pepper, diced
1/2 large onion, chopped
Salt and pepper to taste

Place all ingredients in a pot. Simmer on medium heat until all vegetables are tender, about 20 minutes. If it appears to require more liquid add a bit more juice or water.

Yield: About 6 cups
Total Fat Grams: Less than 1

STIR-FRIED BROCCOLI AND CAULIFLOWER

This dish is delicious with both the broccoli and the cauliflower or just with the broccoli, alone.

1 cup defatted stock
4 tsp. heavy soy sauce
2 tsp. light soy sauce
2 tsp. sugar
2 tsp. fresh ginger, diced
2 tsp. sherry
3 Tbs. cornstarch
1/4 cup white wine or defatted stock
2 cloves garlic, minced
1 large onion, thickly cut
2 cups broccoli flowerets
2 cups cauliflower flowerets

Prepare sauce by combining 1 cup stock, heavy and light soy sauces, sugar, ginger, sherry and cornstarch. Set aside. Heat wok and add 1/4 cup white wine or stock. Add the onion and stir-fry for 4 minutes or until onion becomes translucent. Add broccoli and cauliflower and stir-fry for 3 to 4 minutes or until crisp-tender. Add the sauce and stir-fry until the sauce is thickened. Serve on steamed rice.

Yield: About 6 cups
Total Fat Grams: Less than 1

BROCCOLI AND TOMATOES WITH CHEESE

1 pound broccoli flowerets
2 medium tomatoes, cut in large pieces
3/4 tsp. garlic powder
1/2 tsp. dried oregano
1/4 tsp. Italian seasonings
1/2 cup fat-free cheddar or mozzarella cheese

Steam the broccoli in the microwave in about 4 Tbs. water for about 1 to 2 minutes (each microwave is different) or until bright green and still very crispy. Drain except for 2 Tbs. which you place in a saucepan with the broccoli, tomato, garlic powder, oregano and seasonings. Toss gently and cook, uncovered, over medium-low heat until thoroughly heated, stirring occasionally, about 10 minutes. Sprinkle with cheese. Cover and remove from heat and let stand abut 3 to 4 minutes until the cheese is melted.

Yield: 4 to 5 cups
Total Fat Grams: Traces

SNOW PEAS AND WATER CHESTNUTS

1/4 cup white wine or defatted stock
1 pound fresh pea pods, trimmed
1 Tbs. shallots, minced
1/2 cup water chestnuts, sliced
Salt and freshly ground pepper

Heat wine or stock in a pan. Add all ingredients and stir-fry for about 2 to 3 minutes. Season to taste.

Yield: About 5 cups
Total Fat Grams: 0

PEAS AND WATER CHESTNUTS IN A WOK

1/4 cup white wine or defatted stock
1 small onion, thinly sliced
1/2 tsp. garlic powder
1/2 cup celery, minced
2 packages (10 oz. ea.) frozen peas
1 can (8 oz.) water chestnuts, sliced
1 1/2 tsp. granulated chicken bouillon
1/4 cup water, if necessary
Soy sauce to taste

Sauté the onion, garlic and celery until crisp and tender. Run water over the peas to thaw and add to the pot along with the remaining ingredients except the water. Stir over medium-high heat until all veggies are cooked through and still crisp-tender. Add water, a tablespoon at a time, if pan becomes too dry. Season to taste with soy sauce.

Yield: About 4 cups
Total Fat Grams: Traces

THE VEGETABLE STIR-FRY

This is one of those dishes wherein the imagination of the chef or the variety of vegetables in the refrigerator may determine the ingredients. The recipe may be enlarged or reduced, proportionately, to fit the quantity you desire. Cooked ahead of time, this can be a base stir-fry to which other veggies, poultry or shrimp may be added to enhance the basic vegetables. Frozen vegetables, thawed by running under cold water, then draining, work well, too, to add variety. Once prepared, the stir-fry will store in the refrigerator for about a week, and is a quick and easy dinner if the rice has been cooked beforehand. Then all that's necessary for good eating is a turn in the microwave. For a Szechuan twist (a little hot and spicy!) add Chili Puree with Garlic to taste or crushed red pepper. Both the Oyster sauce and the Chili Puree with Garlic can be found in the Oriental food section of your supermarket or in an Oriental food store. If you decide to use one of the "Stir-Fry" sauces on the grocery shelves, instead of the Oyster sauce, be sure you adjust the fat gram count appropriately.

1/4 cup white wine or defatted stock
2 cloves garlic, minced
1 large onion, thickly sliced
3 ribs celery, sliced diagonally
2 carrots, sliced diagonally
2 cups cabbage, shredded
1/2 cup water chestnuts, sliced
1 cup green bell pepper, sliced
1 cup fresh bean sprouts, rinsed and drained
1/2 pound mushrooms, sliced or thickly cut
3 to 4 Tbs. oyster sauce
Chili Puree with Garlic or crushed red pepper, optional
2 to 3 Tbs. cornstarch
1 to 2 Tbs. cold water
Soy sauce to taste

Each group of vegetables will be stir-fried and removed to a big bowl until the last vegetable is ready, at which time they are all returned to the wok for a toss with the oyster sauce and thickening with cornstarch.

Heat the wine or stock in the wok and heat on high. Add garlic with a pinch of salt. Stir-fry for about 30 seconds and add the onion. Stir fry until the onion is crisp-tender and remove from the wok with a slotted spoon. Stir- fry the carrots and celery until crisp-tender and remove from the wok with slotted spoon. Add stock or wine as necessary to avoid scorching. Combine cabbage, water chestnuts, green pepper and bean sprouts. Stir-fry until crisp-tender and remove from the wok. Replace all ingredients in wok and add mushrooms. At this point you can add broccoli (which has been steamed for about 3 minutes or until crisp-tender), bamboo shoots, thawed frozen peas, or any variety of favorite veggies.

Stir-fry until all vegetables are heated through. Add oyster sauce to taste and Chili Puree with Garlic, if you want it hot. Toss thoroughly. Make a well in the wok bottom, add the cornstarch which has been dissolved in the water, and when it starts to thicken, mix through the vegetables. Serve on steamed rice. Add soy sauce to taste.

Yield: About 8 cups if quantities of vegetables as shown
Total Fat Grams: 3 to 4, if vegetables, only. Add appropriate grams if poultry or seafood is added.

VEGETABLE STEW ITALIAN

1 medium eggplant, pared and cubed
1/4 cup white wine or defatted stock
3 medium onions, thinly sliced
1 rib celery, thinly sliced
2 cups fresh plum tomatoes, peeled and cubed
3 fresh basil leaves or 1/4 tsp. dried basil
Salt and freshly ground black pepper to taste
1 pound potatoes, peeled and sliced
2 green bell peppers, sliced
2 medium zucchini, cut into 1/4 inch slices

Sprinkle salt over the eggplant cubes and set aside. Sauté the onion and celery in the wine until soft. Add the tomatoes, basil leaves, salt and pepper. As soon as the mixture bubbles, add the potatoes and green pepper. When the pepper begins to wilt, add the eggplant. Cook for 5 minutes on medium heat and add the zucchini. Cover and simmer gently for about 15 minutes or until the zucchini is done.

Yield: About 12 cups
Total Fat Grams: Traces

EGGPLANT ITALIANO

1 medium eggplant cut in 3/4 inch slices
1 bottle fat-free Italian dressing
1/2 tsp. dried oregano leaves
1/2 tsp. rosemary
1 cup Basic Marinara Sauce (page 226)
6 Tbs. breadcrumbs (made with fat free bread)

Marinate the eggplant in the dressing with seasonings. Broil the eggplant slices on each side until lightly browned. Spoon Marinara Sauce on the bottom of a 9" x 9" baking pan to cover. Alternate eggplant and Marinara Sauce in layers until all eggplant is used. Place on a lower shelf of the oven and broil until browned and bubbly.

Yield: A 9" x 9" pan
Total Fat Grams: 0

EGGPLANT CASSEROLE WITH WINE

1 large eggplant, cut in half, lengthwise
Olive Oil Pam
1 medium onion, chopped
4 cloves garlic, minced
2 cups mushrooms, halved
1 cup tomatoes, coarsely chopped
1/2 tsp. dried thyme
1 cup dry white wine
1 cup defatted chicken broth or stock
1 pound redskin potatoes, diced, with skins on
Salt and pepper to taste
1/4 cup fresh parsley, chopped
2 Tbs. Parmesan Cheese

Spray Olive Oil Pam on a baking sheet. Score the skin side of the eggplant and place, flat side down, on the baking sheet. Bake at 500° for 10—15 minutes. Remove from the oven and lower heat to 350°. Soften the onion and half the garlic in the microwave in a little water or defatted stock and place in a large pot. Add the mushrooms, tomatoes, thyme, wine, broth, potatoes and the remaining garlic. Add a pinch of salt and simmer for 5 minutes. Without peeling, dice the eggplant. Add the diced eggplant and half the parsley. Cook, stirring, for 10 minutes. Move to an oven-proof baking dish or casserole, cover and bake for 30 to 40 minutes, or until vegetables are tender. Season with salt & pepper to taste. Sprinkle with remaining parsley and Parmesan cheese.

Yield: 8 to 10 cups
Total Fat Grams: 4

EGGPLANT, TOMATO AND COUSCOUS

1/4 cup white wine or defatted stock
1 medium onion, chopped
2 cloves garlic, minced
1 medium eggplant, unpeeled, cubed
1 green bell pepper, thinly sliced
2 cups whole tomatoes, chopped
1 tsp. mixed dried Italian seasonings
4 Tbs. parsley, minced
1 cup water
1 pound cooked couscous

Sauté the onion and garlic in the wine or stock until tender. Add the eggplant and green pepper and cook on medium heat for 10 minutes. Add the remaining ingredients, except couscous, and cook, covered, for 30 minutes. Stir often. Mash the eggplant and cook for another 30 minutes. Spoon over the cooked couscous.

Yield: About 12 cups
Total Fat Grams: Less than 1

EASY EGGPLANT

1/4 cup white wine or defatted stock
1 medium onion, chopped
1 tsp. garlic, minced
2 Tbs. fresh lemon juice
2 1/2 cups canned tomatoes, drained and chopped
1/2 tsp. dried basil
1/2 tsp. paprika
4 dates, minced
1/2 tsp. salt
1 small eggplant, peeled and diced
Fat-free cheese, optional

Sauté the onion and garlic in the wine or stock until crisp-tender. Add remaining ingredients. Bring to a boil, then immediately lower heat to a simmer and cook, covered, for about 15 minutes. May be baked at 375° with addition of Healthy Choice Pasteurized Process Cheese Food or fat-free cheddar cheese placed on top. Bake until cheese melts, about 7 minutes, or serve steamed, as is, on brown rice.

Yield: About 6 cups
Total Fat Grams: 0

SWEET AND SOUR CABBAGE IN A WOK

1/4 cup white wine or defatted stock
1 large onion, sliced
2 carrots, sliced diagonally
1/2 large head of cabbage, sliced
1/2 cup fresh bean sprouts
2 tomatoes, sliced
1/4 cup honey
1/4 cup wine or cider vinegar
2 tsp. cornstarch
Tamari or soy sauce to taste

Sauté the onion in the wine or stock until tender. Add the carrots and stir-fry for about 3 minutes. Add the cabbage and bean sprouts and stir-fry 2 to 3 minutes. Add tomatoes, toss together and add 2 Tbs. water. Cover and cook on medium heat for 10 minutes. Combine the honey and vinegar and stir well. Stir in the cornstarch to dissolve. Add the sauce to the vegetables, stirring, until the sauce thickens and the veggies are glazed. Season with tamari.

Yield: About 6 cups
Total Fat Grams: Less than 1

SWEET AND SOUR BEETS WITH CABBAGE

This tangy dish may be served hot, as a vegetable, with boiled potatoes, or, for a real treat, try it cold with other assorted salads. It's also a great relish side dish with turkey sausage or sandwiches.

2 beets, julienned
1/2 large onion, sliced
1 carrot, julienned
1/2 cup dry red wine
1/4 medium head cabbage, thinly sliced
1 1/2 Tbs. granulated beef bouillon
1/2 cup water
1 1/2 tsp. sugar
1 1/2 Tbs. white wine vinegar
1 tsp. fresh lemon juice
Orange marmalade to taste

Place the beets, onion, carrot and wine in a large pot and cook on medium heat until tender. Add the cabbage and cook until the cabbage is tender. Add the remaining ingredients except the marmalade. Adjust sugar and lemon juice to taste. Add the marmalade to taste.

Yield: About 4 cups
Total Fat Grams: Traces

CABBAGE AND RED POTATOES

2 pounds redskin potatoes, quartered
2 large onions, cut in half and then quartered
4 Tbs. granulated beef or chicken bouillon
1 Tbs. garlic powder
1 head cabbage, heart removed, cut in large pieces
Molly McButter to taste
Salt and pepper to taste

Place potatoes in cold, salted water to cover and bring water to a boil. Cook 5 minutes. Remove most of the water, leaving approximately 1/2 to 3/4 cup of liquid in the pot. Add the remaining ingredients and cook on medium heat until the potatoes and onions are cooked through. If you prefer a buttery flavor, sprinkle some Molly McButter on the mixture and toss. Salt and pepper to taste.

Yield: About 12 cups
Total Fat Grams: Less than 1

CABBAGE AND TOMATOES

This an easy recipe to throw together at the end of a busy day. Microwave a piece of smoked turkey sausage on paper toweling and add to the pot, or serve on the side with mustard, when you're looking for a heartier meal. Be sure to add the fat grams for the addition of the sausage.

4 or 5 small red potatoes, cut in eighths
1/2 head cabbage, cut in large pieces
1 large onion, sliced thick
1/2 cup defatted chicken stock
1 can (15 oz.) White Northern or other white bean
1 can crushed or stewed tomatoes
1/4 tsp. sugar
Salt and pepper to taste

Parboil the potatoes for 5 minutes. Drain the water and add all other ingredients. Simmer, covered, until the onion is cooked through, about 10 minutes.

Yield: About 8 to 10 cups
Total Fat Grams: 2

STRICTLY VEGETARIAN CABBAGE ROLLS

1 cup of white wine or defatted stock
1 rib celery, chopped
1/4 cup red onion, finely chopped
1 1/2 cup tomatoes, finely chopped
1 Tbs. dried basil, or 2 Tbs. fresh basil
1/2 tsp. dried oregano
1 Tbs. rice vinegar
1/2 cup red onion, chopped
1/2 cup chopped mushrooms
1 tsp. garlic, minced
2 Tbs. defatted chicken stock
2 cups cooked rice or barley
1/2 cup tomatoes, chopped
3 Tbs. fat-free bread crumbs
2 tsp. soy sauce
1 tsp. dried parsley, minced
1/2 tsp. curry powder
1/2 tsp. pepper
8 cabbage leaves

Sauté the celery and 1/4 cup onion in the wine or stock until soft. Add 1 1/2 cup tomatoes, basil, oregano and vinegar and simmer, covered, 20 minutes. Remove from the heat and set aside.

Sauté the 1/2 cup onions, mushrooms and garlic in stock 3 to 5 minutes. Mix with the remaining ingredients, except the cabbage leaves, in a large bowl. Blanche the cabbage leaves in boiling water for 3 minutes or until pliable. Drain. Place 1/2 cup mixture in each leaf and roll tightly to enclose the filling. Coat a 9 x 9 baking dish with non-stick spray and place rolls on the dish, seams down. Cover with 1 cup of the sauce. Cover with foil and bake at 400° for 25 to 30 minutes. Serve with the remaining sauce.

Yield: 8 rolls
Total Fat Grams: 1

MASHED POTATOES

Boiling water with 2 tsp. salt
1 pound russet potatoes, peeled and cubed or sliced
1/2 to 3/4 cup skim milk
Molly McButter to taste and salt & pepper to taste

Place the potatoes in boiling salted water to cover. Cook, uncovered on high heat until the potatoes are easily penetrated with a fork, about 10 to 15 minutes. Drain and place the potatoes in a warm bowl. Use a potato ricer, masher, or electric mixer to mash the potatoes. Gradually add the milk to the consistency that pleases you. Add Molly Mcbutter and salt and pepper to taste.

Yield: About 4 cups
Total Fat Grams: 0

MASHED POTATOES WITH SQUASH

1 small butternut squash
2 Tbs. defatted chicken or vegetable stock
4 cups mashed potatoes

Slice the squash in half, remove seeds, peel and cube the meat. Place in a glass or plastic bowl with the stock and microwave on high for 4 to 5 minutes, or until soft. Place in food processor or blender. Blend or process until smooth. Swirl into mashed potatoes.

Yield: About 6 cups
Total Fat Grams: Less than 1

RESTUFFED POTATOES

The potatoes in this recipe must be baked in the oven. If you bake the potatoes in the microwave the skins are too thin and break apart and therefore are impossible to stuff. If time is a problem and the microwave is the only way, prepare as a casserole, instead. The taste is still wonderful!

6 medium to large baking potatoes
3/4 to 1 cup fat free sour cream
1 packet Lipton's Onion Soup Mix
3 oz. Healthy Choice Pasteurized Process Cheese Product

Scrub the potatoes and prick with a fork for even cooking. Place in the oven and bake at 425° for about 1 to 1 1/4 hour or until soft inside when a fork is inserted. Slice the potatoes in half, lengthwise. Scoop out the meat of the potatoes, leaving the skins in tact. Place flesh of potatoes in large mixing bowl and combine with sour cream, onion soup and 2 oz. of cheese, which has been broken up into small pieces (about 1/4"). Toss the mixture to insure even coverage. Stuff the skins with the mixture and place a strip of the remaining cheese on each restuffed half. Bake for 5 minutes or until cheese is melted. These taste good with Baco's, too, and are a taste pleaser without the cheese. The potatoes (without the Baco's) freeze very well and can be prepared ahead of time for a no-fuss company vegetable that tastes elegant. Just reheat in the oven after thawing.

Yield: 12 halves
Total Fat Grams: Traces

SAGE POTATOES

1/4 cup white wine or defatted stock
1 medium onion, sliced
1 Tbs. fresh sage leaves or whole dried leaves, in pieces
2 pounds sliced potatoes with skins, scrubbed
1 can (16 oz.) tomatoes with liquid, sliced
2/3 cup dry white wine
1 package (10 oz.) frozen peas
Salt & freshly ground pepper to taste

Sauté the onion and sage in 1/4 cup wine or stock until the onion is tender. Add the potatoes and toss with the onion for 1 minute, then add tomatoes and wine. Simmer, covered, on low heat for 1 hour or until potatoes are cooked through, stirring occasionally. Add peas and cook 5 minutes more. Season to taste.

Yield: About 8 cups
Total Fat Grams: Less than 1

PARSLEY POTATO PATTIES

4 cups mashed potatoes (leftovers are fine)
2 Tbs. defatted stock or broth
1/2 cup fresh parsley, chopped
1 cup onion, chopped
Paprika, pepper and salt to taste
Spray-on oil, a 2 1/2 second spray

Sauté the onion and parsley in the stock until crisp-tender. Combine with the mashed potatoes and seasoning. Form into flat patties and place on a non-stick cookie sheet treated with Pam. Bake at 375° until golden brown, about 15 to 20 minutes.

Yield: About 12 to 15 patties
Total Fat Grams: 1

BAKED FRENCH FRIES

Go on, you say. They can't be any good! Try 'em...you'll like 'em.

4 potatoes, scrubbed or peeled
Pam or Weight Watcher's Buttery Spray
Salt

Slice potatoes into 1/4 inch strips. Parboil potato strips for 5 minutes. Arrange in single layer on non-stick cookie sheet. Spray with Pam or Buttery Spray, no more than 5 seconds. Sprinkle with salt. Bake at 450° for 8 to 10 minutes or until golden brown. Turn, spray for 2 1/2 seconds to sparsely coat and sprinkle with salt, sparingly. Bake an addition 3 to 5 minutes or until golden.

Yield: About 4 to 6 cups
Total Fat Grams: 3

BAKED YAMS OR SWEET POTATOES

1 yam or sweet potato
Molly McButter to taste
Freshly ground pepper to taste or cinnamon and nutmeg

Scrub and prick the potato. Place in a 400° oven for about 1 hour or until soft inside when a fork is inserted. The size will determine the baking time. An alternative is the microwave. Prepare for baking, place in microwave for 10 to 12 minutes, rotating once or twice, and turning over once, until cooked through and soft inside. Split open and sprinkle Molly McButter to taste. Choose the flavoring you prefer whether it be peppery or aromatic such as cinnamon and nutmeg. Try lime for a taste change.

Yield: 1 potato
Total Fat Grams: Less than 1

BAKED SWEET POTATO RUM CASSEROLE

2 tart apples, cored & diced
Juice of 1/2 fresh lime
2 pounds sweet potatoes or yams, peeled and diced
1/3 cup raisins
2 tsp. Molly McButter
1 1/2 cups apple cider
1/4 to 1/3 cup rum to taste
2 Tbs. honey
Salt to taste
1/2 tsp. ground allspice
1/2 tsp. ground cinnamon
1/4 tsp. ground mace
1 tsp. ground ginger
Spray-on oil or buttery spray

Toss the diced apples with the lime juice, then add the sweet potatoes and raisins. Set aside. Combine the remaining ingredients and heat in a saucepan about 2 minutes. Place potato mixture in a casserole dish sprayed with Weight Watchers Buttery Spray, or other non-stick spray, for 2 1/2 seconds. Pour the sauce over the potato mixture, cover, and bake at 350° for about 45 minutes or until potatoes are thoroughly cooked and glazed.

Yield: About 5 cups
Total Fat Grams: 5

SIMPLE CANDIED SWEET POTATOES

6 peeled yams or sweet potatoes, sliced
Molly McButter
1/2 cup lite maple syrup
2 Tbs. brown sugar
Ground cinnamon, optional

Boil the potato slices until tender, about 15 minutes. Place slices in an oblong, non-stick baking pan. Sprinkle with Molly McButter followed by syrup and a sprinkling of brown sugar and cinnamon. Bake at 350° for 1/2 hour.

Yield: A 9" x 12" pan casserole
Total Fat Grams: 3

Chicken & Turkey

The benefits of eating chicken and turkey make a good case for substituting these flesh foods for beef and pork. The fat grams you'll add to your daily intake will be greatly reduced if you confine your edibles to tasty preparations of poultry with lots of vegetables, grains and legumes. Beef and pork will add four to five times the fat grams per ounce compared to skinless poultry in any recipe, unless only the leanest cuts are used.

The chicken or turkey should always be skinned prior to cooking, and white meat used rather than dark, to attain the maximum benefit. Two ounces of skinless turkey breast, cooked, contains only 1 gram of fat compared to a turkey leg which offers 4 grams for two ounces. Chicken breast, no skin, cooked, will provide 2 grams of fat for two ounces and twice that for dark meat. Be wary of processed turkey and chicken in the guise of low-fat food, since ground turkey, turkey and chicken franks, and turkey and chicken sausage have fat and skin added to the lean meat. READ THE LABELS. Many of these turkey products tout "97% Fat Free" in jumbo lettering. If the fat-gram count per ounce is not spelled out on the label...don't buy it! When buying ground turkey, to authentically cut the fat, purchase turkey breast and have the butcher skin and grind it for you. You know then you are getting 4 grams of fat for a cup of meat, and there are no foreign parts added as filler.

There are so many wonderful recipes, from the down-home variety to the gourmet, utilizing chicken breast and turkey breast. These two forms of flesh food will become a staple for those of you who resist giving up the flavor and texture of meat. The fat grams, as in seafood, are so low that these foods easily fit the requirements of your new low-fat lifestyle. And the preparation of chicken and turkey can be tremendously varied because of the nature of these meats. There are recipes from virtually all over the world that can be enjoyed...spicy or mild; stewed, steamed or roasted; grilled or stir-fried.

The recipes you'll find in the next few pages have been presented to you for ease of preparation and minimal fat content. You will notice that the preceding vegetable, bean and grain recipes are, naturally, lower in fat, and therefore confining the poultry to a few meals a week is a good idea. Try to incorporate the Oriental approach to using meats as a condiment since this manner of food preparation will enhance the flavor of the dish and leave your body and your fat-gram count in good shape.

CHICKEN-SGHETTI

10 cups basic Marinara Sauce (page 226)
1 pound white meat chicken, skinned, bone-in

During the initial preparation of the Marinara Sauce, when the sauce is ready for the 4 hours of simmer, place the raw, cleaned, skinned, trimmed chicken parts in the sauce and continue to cook, partially covered, on a low simmer. After 3 hours or so, the meat will fall off the bones. Remove the bones, refrigerate the sauce overnight, skim any fat which may have accumulated at the top of the sauce (if the fat on the chicken breasts had been trimmed away, there won't be any to skim), reheat and serve.

If the Marinara sauce is already completed and has been stored in the refrigerator or freezer, bring it back to medium heat, place the chicken in the sauce, and simmer on low, partially covered, for about 2 hours, or until the meat falls off the bone. Continue as above. Serve on cooked pasta.

Yield: About 12 cups
Total Fat Grams: 25

CHICKEN BREAST MARSALA

4 boneless, skinned chicken breast halves (4 oz. ea.)
Olive Oil Pam
Garlic powder
1 medium onion, thinly sliced
2 tsp. dried oregano
1/2 cup Marsala wine
1/2 pound sliced mushrooms
Freshly ground pepper

Heat a non-stick skillet and spray with Pam. Sprinkle both sides of the chicken breasts with garlic powder. Place breasts in the hot pan and sear on both sides to seal in the juices. Add the remaining ingredients and poach gently until chicken is cooked through, about 10-15 minutes. Season with freshly ground pepper.

Yield: 4 chicken breasts
Total Fat Grams: 17

CHICKEN WITH EGGPLANT AND TOMATOES

1 eggplant, sliced, with skin
Salt & pepper
1 green bell pepper, sliced
2 large onions, sliced
Spray-on oil
1/4 cup defatted chicken stock
4 skinless, boneless chicken breast halves (4 oz. ea.)
2 cups tomato juice
2 cans (16 oz. ea.) whole tomatoes, drained and quartered

Salt and pepper eggplant slices and let stand 15 minutes. Brown chicken in spray-on oil in a large pan, turning frequently, for about 5 minutes. Add stock and cook 5 minutes more. Remove chicken and set aside. Add green pepper and onions and simmer until soft. Return the chicken, add the tomato juice and 1/2 tsp. each salt and pepper. Rinse the eggplant and pat dry. Add to the chicken mixture and simmer, covered 20 minutes. Add tomatoes and cook 5 minutes more. May be served on steamed rice or pasta.

Yield: 4 chicken breasts with about 8 cups eggplant and sauce
Total Fat Grams: 18

QUICK CHICKEN TOMATO

2 skinless, boneless chicken breast halves (4 oz. ea.)
Olive Oil Pam
1 medium onion, sliced
1/2 cup mushrooms, sliced
1/2 tsp. garlic powder
1 can (16 oz.) whole tomatoes with juice
1 Tbs. mixed dry Italian seasonings
3 Tbs. white wine, optional

Spray the Pam in a hot saucepan or wok and sear the chicken for about 3 minutes on each side. Add all remaining ingredients and cook, uncovered, on medium heat until juices from the tomatoes are reduced by half and thickened, breaking up tomatoes as they cook. Test the chicken for doneness. Add the white wine when the chicken is cooked through, if desired. Season with salt and pepper to taste.

Yield: 2 chicken breasts with about 3 cups sauce
Total Fat Grams: 10

CHICKEN VERMOUTH

4 skinless, boneless chicken breast halves (4 oz. ea.)
Salt
1/4 cup dry vermouth
2 Tbs. fresh lemon juice
Freshly ground black pepper

Pound the chicken breasts with a mallet or flat side of a cleaver until about double in size. Pat dry with paper towels. Place a non-stick pan on high heat and sprinkle with salt. When hot the salt will turn light brown. Add the chicken and cook until lightly browned on both sides. Add the vermouth and cook, covered for 1 minute. Reduce heat, uncover and cook until the chicken is white through center. Sprinkle with lemon juice and season to taste with salt and pepper.

Yield: 4 chicken breasts
Total Fat Grams: 16

CHICKEN & TOMATO CURRY

4 skinless, boneless chicken breast halves (4 oz. ea.)
1/4 cup white wine or stock
1 medium onion, chopped
1 green bell pepper, chopped
1 clove garlic, minced
1 tsp. curry powder or more to taste
2 cans (16 oz. ea.) tomatoes with juice, chopped
1/2 cup tomato juice
1/2 cup raisins

Brown the chicken breasts in a non-stick pan, on both sides. Set aside. Sauté the onion, green pepper and garlic in the wine or stock in the same pan until tender. Add the curry powder and mix. Add the tomatoes and juice and heat for 2 minutes. Transfer the mixture to a baking dish. Place the chicken in the baking dish and spoon some of the sauce on top. Bake, covered, at 350° for 30 minutes, sprinkle raisins on top and bake for 10 minutes more. Serve on rice.

Yield: 4 chicken breasts with about 4 cups sauce
Total Fat Grams: 16

EASY CURRIED CHICKEN

1 can Healthy Request Cream of Mushroom soup, undiluted
2 1/2 cups boiling water
2 cups defatted chicken stock
2 1/2 cups uncooked white rice
2 tsp. curry powder
1/2 tsp. salt
4 boneless, skinless chicken breast halves (4 oz. ea.)

Bring all liquid ingredients to a boil. Add rice, curry and salt and bring to boil again. Place chicken breasts in baking pan and cover with rice mixture. Cover pan tightly with aluminum foil and bake at 350° for 30 minutes. Remove, let stand 10 minutes, serve.

Yield: 4 chicken breasts with 5 cups rice
Total Fat Grams: 22

CHICKEN PROVENÇAL

8 skinless, boneless chicken breast halves (4 oz. ea.)
Spray-on oil
2 Tbs. white wine or defatted stock
1 large onion, chopped
4 cloves garlic, sliced thin
1 red bell pepper cut in 1 inch squares
1 medium zucchini, halved and cut in 1/4 inch slices
1 small eggplant cut in 1/4 inch slices and then cut in quarters
1 can (28 oz.) tomatoes, drained and chopped
1/4 tsp. dried basil
1/4 tsp. thyme
1/4 tsp. dried oregano, crushed
2 Tbs. dried parsley, minced

Place the chicken in a large pan treated with spray and brown on both sides. Set aside. Add the wine or stock to the pan and sauté the onion and garlic until tender. Add the green pepper and cook for 5 minutes. Add the zucchini and cook 5 minutes more. Transfer the veggies to the bowl with the chicken and sauté the eggplant in the pan 5 to 7 minutes or until golden. Replace the chicken and vegetables to the pan and add the tomatoes and herbs. Lower the heat to moderate and cook, covered 15 minutes or until the chicken is cooked through. Transfer to a heated platter and sprinkle with parsley.

Yield: 8 chicken breasts with about 6 cups vegetables and sauce
Total Fat Grams: 33

STIR-FRIED CHICKEN WITH GREEN BEANS

2 boneless, skinless chicken breast halves (4 oz. ea.)
1 tsp. cornstarch
1/2 cup defatted chicken or vegetable stock
1 Tbs. soy sauce
1/2 tsp. sesame oil
3 Tbs. white wine or defatted stock
1/2 pound young green beans
1/4 pound sliced mushrooms
1 can (8 oz.) bamboo shoots, drained
Freshly ground black pepper

Flatten the chicken breasts until about 1/4 inch thick. Slice into 1/4 inch strips. Set aside. Mix together the cornstarch, 1/2 cup stock, soy sauce and sesame oil. Set aside. Place the wok over high heat and add 3 Tbs. wine or stock. Add the beans and stir-fry for about 3 to 4 minutes. Add mushrooms and stir-fry 1 to 2 minutes, until green beans and mushrooms are crisp-tender. Set aside and keep warm in a covered bowl. Place chicken strips in the wok and stir-fry until firm and white through center. Add sauce and bean/mushroom mixtures which had been set aside and stir-fry until sauce thickens. Season to taste with pepper and serve on steamed rice.

Yield: About 6 cups
Total Fat Grams: 12

SZECHUAN CHICKEN AND GREEN PEPPERS

This is one of David's favorites. It takes about 15 minutes to get the ingredients together, the marinade made and the chicken cubed. We use pre-frozen, boneless chicken breasts which we always have stocked in the freezer just for this type dish. After using the 30 minutes to heat up the rice (which, of course, was frozen), and set the table, etc. the preparation of this delicious Oriental delight is a mere 10 minutes. Prepare a stir-fry of mixed veggies to go with this and guests will think they're in a fine Chinese restaurant!

2 Tbs. Chili Puree with Garlic
1 tsp. white rice vinegar
1/2 tsp. sugar
1 Tbs. light soy sauce
1 tsp. sesame oil
1 Tbs. sherry or white wine
1 clove garlic, minced
1 Tbs. cornstarch
2 boneless, skinless chicken breast halves (4 oz. ea.), cubed
2 medium green bell peppers, cut in 3/4 inch squares
1 to 2 dried red hot peppers

Combine the Chili Puree with Garlic and the sugar. Set aside. Combine the soy sauce, sesame oil, sherry, garlic and cornstarch. Marinate the chicken cubes in the soy sauce mixture for 30 minutes. After the 30 minutes, place the chicken in a baking dish in one layer and microwave for 3 1/2 minutes on high. Stir and microwave for another 3 minutes or until cooked through. Place the green peppers in a wok which has been treated with non-stick spray. Stir-fry peppers with Chili Puree and sugar mixture for 1 minute. Add the red hot peppers (if you like it hot) and stir-fry 2 minutes more. Add the chicken and stir-fry until the green peppers are crisp-tender and the chicken and peppers are thoroughly tossed with sauce. Serve on steamed rice. This is a Szechuan dish and can make the tears flow.

Yield: About 5 cups
Total Fat Grams: 14

CHICKEN WITH PLUM SAUCE

4 skinless, boneless chicken breast halves (4 oz. ea.)
1 Tbs. soy sauce
1 Tbs. sherry
1/4 cup white wine
1 large onion, chopped
1 clove garlic, minced
1/2 tsp. ginger root, minced
1 large green bell pepper, cut in thin strips
1/2 cup water
1 Tbs. Oriental plum sauce
Soy sauce to taste

Pound and flatten the chicken breasts. Cut lengthwise into narrow strips. In a small bowl, combine the soy sauce and sherry. Add the chicken strips and set aside to marinate for 15 minutes. Place a wok over high heat and add the wine or stock. Stir-fry the onion about 1 minute, add the garlic, ginger root and bell pepper and stir-fry until the pepper is crisp-tender, about 2 minutes. Push veggies to the side of the wok. Add the chicken, reserving marinade. Stir-fry chicken until cooked through, about 2 minutes. Add water, reserved marinade and plum sauce. Stir-fry until slightly thickened. Season with soy sauce. Serve on steamed rice.

Yield: About 6 cups
Total Fat Grams: 16

BARI'S TURKEY TETRAZZINI

4 oz. thin spaghetti, cooked according to pkg. directions
2 Tbs. white wine
1/2 onion, minced
4 oz. sliced mushrooms
1 cup defatted chicken stock
1 can Healthy Request Cream of Mushroom Soup, undiluted
1/4 cup dry vermouth
Salt and pepper to taste
6 Tbs. fat-free grated Parmesan cheese
2 cups diced, cooked turkey breast

Cook and drain the spaghetti and set aside in a colander after rinsing. Sauté the onions and mushrooms in the wine until soft. Combine all other ingredients except the turkey and spaghetti. Stir well to blend and cook, uncovered, until hot, about 4 to 5 minutes. Add the turkey and spaghetti, toss lightly to cover. Simmer, covered, until piping hot, about 6 to 8 minutes.

Yield: About 4 cups
Total Fat Grams: 14

TURKEY AND BEAN SKILLET DINNER

1/4 cup white wine or defatted stock
1 medium onion, chopped
4 carrots, chopped
1 pound ground turkey, thawed
1/2 cup tomato sauce
1/2 tsp. oregano
2 cups canned beans such as red, navy or chickpeas, drained
Salt and freshly ground pepper to taste
1/2 cup fresh parsley, chopped

Sauté the onion and carrots in the wine in a 12-inch skillet about 5 minutes. Add the turkey and stir-fry, breaking up the meat to remove all pink. Place the meat in a strainer to drain the juices which have resulted from searing the meat. Replace the meat in the pan and add the tomato sauce, oregano and beans. Season to taste. Continue to cook on high, stirring for a few more minutes until hot through, add parsley and serve on pasta or rice.

Yield: About 8 cups
Total Fat Grams: 20, if well drained. 34, if not drained.

BROCCOLI-TURKEY WITH RICE

If this recipe looks familiar to you, you may remember seeing this as the Broccoli Rice recipe on page 169. Wonderful as a veggie, here you have a casserole that's a snap to prepare and will satisfy the flesh-eaters among you. Chicken may be substituted for the turkey. Fresh or frozen green beans may be substituted for the broccoli.

1 cup raw turkey breast, sliced in quarter-inch strips
4 cups broccoli flowerets, fresh, or frozen and thawed
1 large onion, thinly sliced
2 cans Healthy Request Cream of Mushroom soup, undiluted
2 Tbs. Worcestershire sauce
2 cups Uncle Ben's Converted Rice, uncooked
4 cups boiling water
3 Tbs. granulated chicken bouillon
3/4 cup Healthy Choice Grated Cheddar Cheese, separated

Mix all ingredients, except cheese, in a large casserole. Bake at 350°, covered, for 1 hour. Remove from oven, add 1/2 cup cheese and mix through. Sprinkle the remaining cheese on the top and return to the oven for 10 minutes or until cheese has melted.

Yield: 10 cups
Total Fat Grams: 15

NUKED TURKEY & RICE BAKE

This quickie cook-up is similar to the Broccoli-Turkey with Rice, preceding, yet is a microwave wonder that cooks in 8 to 10 minutes with the ingredients already prepared and left over from other cookings, or stored in the freezer for just such a night as this. If you purchased your turkey breast, cubed and froze it, raw, a few minutes in the microwave will separate the cubes. Then cook in one layer in the microwave for about 5 minutes on high, stir and microwave for another 5 minutes or until done.

Rice, of course, is always frozen, in packets, in your freezer ready to add to any of these one-dish meals after a microwaving to thaw.

1 1/2 cups cooked rice
3 cups turkey breast, cooked and cubed
1/2 cup celery, chopped
1/4 cup onion, chopped
1 can (8 oz.) sliced water chestnuts, drained
1 can Healthy Request Cream of Mushroom Soup, undiluted
1/2 cup defatted chicken stock or broth
2 Tbs. chopped pimento
2 Tbs. soy sauce
1 jar (4 oz.) chopped mushrooms, drained

Combine all the ingredients in a 3 quart microwave-proof casserole. Cover with a tight lid or plastic wrap. Microwave on high for 8 to 10 minutes or until hot through, stirring occasionally.

Yield: About 6 cups
Total Fat Grams: 14

TURKEY BURGERS

So you wanted to know how you would satisfy that yearning for a big, fat hamburger with all the trimmings! Well, try this one and see how you do.

1 pound ground turkey
1 medium onion, chopped
1/2 tsp. garlic powder
1/2 cup fat-free bread crumbs
2 egg whites, lightly beaten
1/4 to 1/2 cup barbecue sauce
Salt and pepper to taste

Combine all ingredients. Shape into burgers and grill or broil. Make the hamburgers the size and shape you prefer and dress for serving as you would any burgers you enjoy.

Yield: 4 large or 6 medium burgers
Total Fat Grams: 32, with no consideration made for loss of fat in drippings

DAVID'S FAMOUS CHILI

This chili is a winner when prepared with the Wick Fowler pre-mix. It was good eating with other brands but the seasonings are different and it didn't get the raves. If you can't find the Wick Fowler 2-Alarm Chili Kit, write to Caliente Chili, Inc., P.O. Drawer 5340, Austin, Texas 78763, and they'll tell you where to find it.

1/4 cup white wine or defatted stock
2 large onions, coarsely chopped
2 pounds butcher-ground turkey breast
4 cans (16 oz. ea.) whole tomatoes with juice, chopped
1/2 cup tomato sauce, optional
1 package Wick Fowler 2-Alarm Chili Kit
64 oz. canned kidney beans, drained

Sauté the onions in white wine or stock until translucent. Add the turkey and cook, breaking up meat, until brown and no pink color remains. Drain well. Add tomatoes. If you like a looser, runnier chili add the tomato sauce. Add the seasonings from the Chili Kit, adjusting the red pepper packet to taste. If you like it medium spicy, use it all. Omit the masa flour if you like your chili juicy. If you like a thicker chili, add the masa flour according to package directions. Simmer, covered for 45 minutes, stirring occasionally. Add the kidney beans, cover and simmer 45 minutes more, stirring occasionally. Serve at once.

Yield: About 14 cups
Total Fat Grams: 40. Make necessary change if pre-ground turkey is used: about 58, or 72, if not drained

KIMMIE'S CHILI QUICKIE

1 pound butcher-ground turkey
1 large onion, chopped
1 tsp. chili powder (more to taste)
1 tsp. Mrs. Dash Mexican Seasoning
4 oz. beer, optional
1/4 cup fat-free salsa
2 cans Old El Paso Mexe-Beans
1 can (16 oz.) stewed tomatoes

Brown the turkey, leaving no pink meat, in a non-stick pan. Drain well. Add the onion and stir-fry until the onion is soft. Add the remaining ingredients. Cook on medium heat for 30 to 45 minutes, stirring occasionally.

Yield: About 8 cups
Total Fat Grams: 16

SWEET TURKEY ORIENTAL

1 1/2 pounds fresh turkey breast, skinned & cubed
1 cup soy sauce
1 cup pineapple chunks
1 can (8 oz.) mandarin oranges
1 onion, cut in 1 inch squares
1 green bell pepper, cut in 1 inch squares
1 cup fresh mushrooms, sliced
1 cup fresh snow peas
1/2 cup water chestnuts, sliced
1/2 cup bamboo shoots
1/3 cup pineapple juice
10 to 12 cherry tomatoes
1 cup frozen peas, thawed
3 cups cooked white rice

Marinate the turkey in soy sauce for 1 hour, then stir-fry in a hot wok for 1 minute, adding 2 Tbs. pineapple juice as the turkey starts to cook. Stir-fry for about 4 minutes. Add the onion. When the onion is translucent, add the green pepper and snow peas, stir-frying an additional 2 minutes. Add remaining ingredients and stir-fry about 2 minutes more. Add the white rice and toss until the rice is hot.

Yield: About 15 cups
Total Fat Grams: 17

SICILIAN TURKEY

1/4 cup white wine or defatted stock
1 pound raw turkey breast, cut in thin strips
1 medium onion, diced
1 green bell pepper, diced
1 medium zucchini, diced
2 large tomatoes, chopped
2 tsp. mixed dry Italian seasonings
Olive Oil Pam
1 Tbs. fresh lemon juice
Salt and freshly ground black pepper to taste

Heat the wine or stock and add the turkey strips. Stir over high heat until the meat is cooked through, about 3 to 4 minutes. Set the turkey aside. With the pan on medium heat, add the onion and bell pepper, a dash more wine or stock if needed, and sauté for about 1 minute. Add the zucchini and tomatoes, cover and steam for about 2 to 3 minutes or until the vegetables are crisp-tender. Stir in the Italian seasonings, spray for 2-1/2 seconds with Olive Oil Pam and add the lemon juice. Stir and season to taste with salt and pepper. Add the turkey strips. Simmer until all ingredients are hot through. Serve on rice or pasta.

Yield: About 6 cups
Total Fat Grams: 10

SEAFOOD

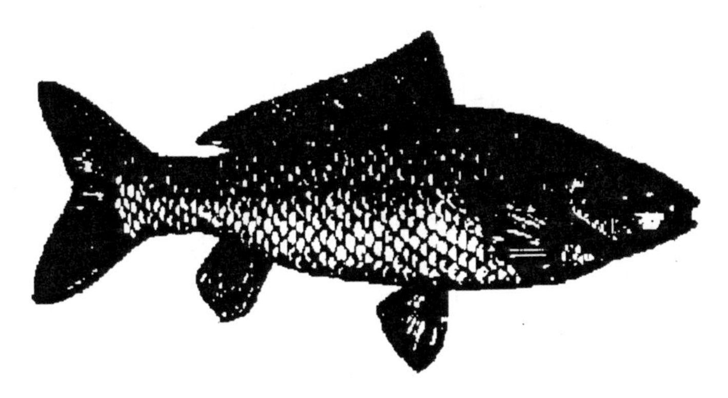

The shellfish and seafood we savor in this low-fat lifestyle are truly delightful and adapt well to low-fat preparation. You will find a number of some of my favorites in this section which I hope will become favorites of yours, too.

Preparing fish and seafood at home may be intimidating to many people because of the delicacy of the flesh and the tendency to overcook which causes the tender meat to become tough and rubbery. On the other hand, there are definite advantages to using care when preparing seafood since undercooking may cause greater problems than overcooking. However, the enjoyment you'll derive from learning to properly purchase and prepare these morsels from the sea is well worth the investment you'll make in experimentation and practice.

Any seafood must be purchased when it is fresh. Choose a market where there is a bustling business so the fish you're buying has not been sitting in the refrigerated showcase too long. Whole fish should have clear eyes which do not have a milky or sunken look. The gills should be bright red and never muddy-colored. The flesh should be unmarred and sufficiently firm and elastic that your finger will not leave an indentation. The flesh of steaks and fillets should be bright and shiny. Fresh fish should not have a strong, unpleasant odor but rather an often cucumberlike scent. Shrimp should be firm and smell fresh with no hint of the odor of ammonia which indicates spoilage. Be sure to replace seafood in the refrigerator no more than two hours after purchase to avoid bacterial growth.

When preparing fish you want the look of transparency to change to opaque and the flesh to flake with a fork. Shrimp should turn pink and, if shelled, the body of the shrimp will curl.

Many of the recipes you see calling for chicken are easily adaptable to shellfish, especially shrimp. Certainly this should be a consideration when looking for a new, exciting dinner idea whether it be an Oriental recipe or Italian. A perfect example of this is the recipe which starts off our seafood section, Shrimp and Clam Marinara. Serve this dish with crusty, fat-free French bread and a fresh, crispy salad and you'll take a place of honor in your friends' eyes as a master chef!

SHRIMP AND CLAM MARINARA

This sauce, which is served on pasta, is the same Marinara you used in the Chicken-Sghetti (page 287). Here, with the shrimp and clams, it brings you a different way of looking at your pasta. Try it with fresh clams added and placed on top for a "company" touch. Be sure to scrub the shells of the clams with a stiff brush in cold running water to clean off any sand and debris.

Without the fresh clams this is an easy 15 minute dish for any busy day.

6 cups Basic Marinara Sauce (page 226)
1/2 pound large or medium shrimp, peeled and deveined
1 can (6 1/2 oz.) chopped clams or whole baby clams
24 to 30 fresh baby clams in the shell (optional)
Cooked pasta of your choice

Heat the sauce which has been refrigerated overnight or thawed from the freezer. When the sauce is heated through, 10 minutes before serving, add the shrimp and canned clams with 1 to 2 Tbs. of the clam juices to taste. Simmer uncovered for about 5 to 7 minutes, or until the shrimp are cooked through. Serve at once on the cooked, reheated pasta.

If fresh clams in the shell are used, place them in the sauce, after cleaning, with the other ingredients and cover. Check in 5 minutes. If the shells are beginning to open they are cooked and it's time to check the shrimp. When the clams are ready the shrimp should be cooked through.

Yield: About 12 cups
Total Fat Grams: 5 (fresh clams: approximately 1 gram for 2 medium clams)

SHRIMP WITH TOMATOES AND HOT PEPPERS

3 Tbs. white wine or defatted stock
1 small onion, chopped
1 small clove garlic, minced
1 can (12 oz.) Italian plum tomatoes undrained
1/8 to 1/4 tsp. dried red pepper flakes
1 1/2 pounds medium shrimp, peeled and deveined
Salt and freshly ground pepper to taste

Sauté the onion and garlic in the wine or stock until soft. Stir in the tomatoes with juices and red pepper. Boil, breaking up tomatoes, until the liquid is reduced by 1/2. Add shrimp, stirring, until the shrimp curl and turn pink. Season to taste with salt and pepper. Serve on Red Rice (page 224) or steamed white rice.

Yield: About 6 cups
Total Fat Grams: 6

SHRIMP PARMIGIANO

1 tsp. olive oil
1 Tbs. dry white wine
1 pound large shrimp, peeled and deveined
2 Tbs. garlic powder
1 tsp. dried mixed Italian seasonings
3 cups Marinara Sauce (page 226), at room temperature
1 cup Healthy Choice Fat Free Grated Mozzarella Cheese
Fat free Parmesan cheese to taste

Heat a skillet or wok and add olive oil and wine. When hot, add the shrimp and sprinkle with the garlic powder and Italian seasoning, stirring constantly for 20 to 30 seconds, or until the shrimp starts to pink up. Do not thoroughly cook. Remove from heat and place shrimp in oven-proof baking dish. Pour Marinara Sauce over the shrimp and bake at 375° for 20 minutes. Sprinkle the mozzarella cheese evenly over sauce and reheat for about 5 to 8 minutes or until the cheese melts. Serve with Parmesan cheese.

Yield: 4 to 5 cups
Total Fat Grams: 9

SHRIMP CREOLE

2 Tbs. white wine or defatted stock
1/2 cup onion, chopped
1/2 cup green bell pepper, chopped
1/2 cup celery, diced
1 clove garlic, minced
1 can (16 oz.) whole tomatoes, crushed
1 can (8 oz.) tomato sauce
1 Tbs. Worcestershire sauce
1 tsp. salt
1 tsp. sugar
1/2 tsp. chili powder
Hot pepper sauce to taste
1 Tbs. cornstarch
2 Tbs. water
1 pound shrimp, cooked

Sauté the onion, green pepper, celery and garlic in the wine or stock until tender, in a 2 to 3 quart pot. Add all ingredients except the cornstarch, water and shrimp. Simmer, covered, for 8 minutes, stirring occasionally. Dissolve cornstarch in the water and stir into the casserole. Cook, uncovered, for 4 minutes stirring occasionally. Add the shrimp. Cook about 3 minutes, until the shrimp is hot through. Serve on steamed rice.

Yield: About 5 cups
Total Fat Grams: 5

EASY SHRIMP CREOLE

1/4 cup white wine or defatted stock
1 medium onion, chopped
1 small green bell pepper, chopped
1 can (6 oz.) tomato paste
1 can (16 oz.) whole tomatoes with juice, chopped
1 pound medium shrimp, cleaned and deveined
Salt and freshly ground pepper

Sauté the onion and green pepper in the wine or stock until soft. Mix the juice of the tomatoes with the paste and add to the sauté with the tomatoes. Simmer for 5 to 7 minutes. Add the shrimp and cook until the shrimp turn pink and are cooked through. Season with salt and pepper and serve on rice.

Yield: About 5 cups
Total Fat Grams: 4

SWEET AND SOUR SHRIMP

1/4 cup sugar
2 Tbs. cornstarch
1 can (13 1/2 oz.) pineapple chunks, reserve liquid
1/4 cup vinegar
2 tsp. soy sauce
2 ribs celery, sliced
4 green onions with tops, sliced
1/2 medium green bell pepper, thinly sliced
1 large tomato, cut in eighths
1/2 pound shrimp, peeled and deveined

Combine the sugar and cornstarch in a saucepan. Add enough water to the pineapple juices to measure 1 cup. Stir together the pineapple liquid, vinegar and soy sauce and gradually add to the sugar and cornstarch mixture, cooking over low heat until thickened, stirring constantly. Stir the pineapple, celery, onions and green pepper into the sauce mixture. Fold in the tomato and shrimp. Heat until the shrimp is cooked through. Season with additional soy sauce. Serve over steamed rice.

Yield: About 4 cups
Total Fat Grams: 3

ORIENTAL SHRIMP IN GARLIC SAUCE

3 Tbs. white wine or defatted stock
1 small onion, chopped
1 tsp. ginger root, grated
4 cloves garlic, sliced
5 to 6 Shitake mushrooms, soaked 30 minutes and sliced
1 cup frozen peas, thawed
1 pound shrimp, cooked
1/2 cup chicken broth
2 tsp. soy sauce
1/2 tsp. salt
1 Tbs. cornstarch,
2 Tbs. water

Sauté the onion, ginger root and garlic in the wine or stock for 1 to 2 minutes. Add the mushrooms and peas and stir-fry 2 to 3 minutes. Add the shrimp and continue to stir-fry 1 to 2 minutes. Dissolve the cornstarch in the water and combine with the broth, soy sauce, and salt. Add to the shrimp in the pan or wok and heat until the sauce boils and thickens. Serve at once on steamed rice.

Yield: About 4 cups
Total Fat Grams: 4

SWEET AND SOUR SHRIMP II

1 medium onion, sliced thin
1 medium green bell pepper, cut into strips
4 Tbs. dry white wine or defatted chicken stock
1/4 cup rice vinegar
1 Tbs. soy sauce
2 tsp. cornstarch
1/2 tsp. ginger
1 can (8 oz.) juice-packed, crushed pineapple
1 pound shrimp, peeled, deveined and cooked
1/4 cup sugar

Sauté the onion and green pepper in the wine or stock in a wok, until the onion is transparent. In separate bowl, combine the vinegar, soy sauce, cornstarch and ginger, add the pineapple, and add the mixture to the wok. Simmer until the mixture thickens. Stir in the shrimp and sugar and heat thoroughly, only until the shrimp are heated through. Serve on steamed rice.

Yield: 5 cups
Total Fat Grams: 4

SHRIMP AND MUSHROOMS

1/4 cup white wine
1 small onion, thinly sliced
1 clove garlic, minced
4 fresh basil leaves or 1/2 tsp. dried basil
1 pound shrimp, peeled and deveined
1/2 pound mushrooms, sliced
1/4 cup dry white wine

Sauté the onion and garlic in 1/4 cup wine until tender. Add the shrimp, mushrooms and basil and toss over medium-high heat until cooked through. Serve on pasta or with vegetables.

Yield: About 3 cups
Total Fat Grams: 4

SHRIMP WITH CHICKEN AND CAULIFLOWER

1/2 cup chicken broth or defatted stock
1 Tbs. soy sauce
2 Tbs. chili sauce
1 Tbs. cornstarch,
2 Tbs. water
1/4 cup dry white wine
1 cup cauliflower flowerets
2 Tbs. white wine
1 cup frozen peas, thawed
1 pound shrimp, cooked
1/2 pound chicken breast, cubed and cooked
2 scallions, sliced lengthwise

Combine the broth, soy sauce, chili sauce, the cornstarch which has been dissolved in the water, and 1/4 cup wine. Set aside. Cook the cauliflower for about 3 to 4 minutes in boiling water until just crispy-tender. Set aside. Heat 2 Tbs. wine or stock in a wok or large pan. Add the cauliflower and stir-fry 1 to 2 minutes. Add the peas and stir-fry 1 minute. Add the shrimp, chicken and scallions and stir-fry until heated through. Add the sauce mixture and boil until the sauce thickens. Serve on steamed rice or cooked vermicelli.

Yield: About 6 cups
Total Fat Grams: 12

SHRIMP AND SPINACH

4 Tbs. dry white wine or defatted chicken stock
1 pound medium shrimp, peeled and deveined
1 Tbs. garlic powder
1/2 cup defatted chicken stock
1 pound fresh spinach, cleaned and stemmed
1 tsp. olive oil
1 tsp. celery seed

Heat the wine or stock and toss the shrimp with the garlic powder for about 2 minutes. Add the additional stock and the remaining ingredients. Cook on high until the spinach is wilted and the shrimp is cooked through. If you like lots of garlic, increase the amount or use fresh, minced. Serve on pasta or rice.

Yield: 8 cups
Total Fat Grams: 9

THAI SHRIMP WITH BASIL

This dish is divine: aromatic, because of the wonderful fresh basil, and very hot, due to the chilies. It's very soupy and requires lots of steamed rice. It's truly worth trying!

1 pound shrimp, peeled and deveined
1 bunch basil (2 cups fresh leaves)
2 cloves garlic, minced
2 or 3 hot red or green chilies (serrano or fresh jalapeño), seeds removed, sliced thin
4 green onions
1 tsp. peanut oil
1/2 cup + 2 Tbs. defatted chicken stock
2 Tbs. fish sauce
2 Tbs. soy sauce
1 tsp. sugar
Hot steamed rice

Wash, dry and stem the basil. Mince the white part of the green onions and cut the green part into 1 inch pieces. Set aside. Heat the wok over high heat. Add the oil and 2 Tbs. stock. Add the white part of the green onion, only, along with the garlic and chilies. Cook 10 seconds. Add the shrimp and cook for 20 seconds. Add the fish sauce, soy, sugar, stock and the green part of the onion. Bring to a boil. Stir in the basil and cook for 20 seconds. Serve with the rice.

Yield: 4 to 5 cups
Total Fat Grams: 9

GUISEPPE'S CLAM SAUCE

1/2 cup liquid Butter Buds
1 tsp. olive oil
1 tsp. garlic, minced fine
1 can (6 1/2 oz.) chopped clams, reserve broth
3 Tbs. fresh parsley, minced fine

Place all ingredients into a saucepan, except the broth. Heat to simmering. If you prefer a more pronounced clam taste add broth to taste.

Yield: 1 cup
Total Fat Grams: 5

SHRIMP, OYSTER AND CLAM BOIL

1 pound yams or sweet potatoes
2 medium russet potatoes
3/4 cup water
2 Tbs. crab or shrimp boil seasoning, or pickling spice
1/4 tsp. salt
1 pound clams, shells scrubbed under cold running water
6 oysters, shells scrubbed under cold running water
2 large, fresh ears of corn, husked and halved crosswise
Weight Watchers Buttery Spray
4 oz. small shrimp (36-42 count) in the shells

Peel the yams and cut in half, lengthwise, then cut into 1 1/2 inch pieces. Cut the peeled russet potatoes in half lengthwise and then into 2 inch pieces. Place in a large heavy-bottomed pot over medium-high heat. Add the water, 1 Tbs. of the crab boil and the salt. Cover and bring to a boil. Reduce the heat to medium and cook until the potatoes are nearly soft through, about 10 minutes.

Add the clams, oysters and corn, in that order so that the corn is on top. Sprinkle the remaining crab boil over the corn and spray for 2 1/2 seconds with Weight Watchers Buttery Spray. Cover and bring back to a boil. Cook until the corn is cooked, the clam shells open, and the oysters are either open or very close to it, about 7 minutes. Discard any clams or oysters that do not open. Add the shrimp around and over the corn. Cook until the shrimp turn pink, about 4 to 5 minutes. Remove from the heat and serve in the pot.

Yield: About 12 cups
Total Fat Grams: 8

BOUILLABAISSE

The fish used for this dish should be firm-fleshed fish such as cod or grouper. Other shellfish, such as oysters and mussels may be added to the pot along with the lobster, shrimp and clams. In fact, this is the classic recipe and may be adapted by you according to your individual tastes in the realm of seafood. The only difference you'll find here is the oils are missing.

1/4 cup white wine or defatted stock
1 medium onion, chopped
1 carrot, chopped
1 clove garlic, minced
1 pound fish fillets, cut in 3-inch pieces
3 lobster tails, left in shells
1/2 pound medium shrimp, peeled and deveined
3 cups water
1 bay leaf
1 can (8 Oz.) tomato sauce
1 dozen clams, shells scrubbed under cold running water
1 cup wine or broth
1 tsp. fresh lemon juice
1 tsp. dried parsley
1/2 tsp. salt
1/4 tsp. saffron thread or curry powder

Sauté the onion, carrot and garlic in wine or stock until tender. Add the fish fillets, lobster tails, shrimp, water, bay leaf, tomato sauce and clams and simmer about 5 to 7 minutes. Add the remaining ingredients and simmer until all seafood is cooked through and the clams have opened, about 7 minutes more. Discard any clams which have not opened.

Yield: About 16 cups
Total Fat Grams: 7

QUICKIE CLAM AND RICE DINNER

4 Tbs. white wine or defatted stock
4 Tbs. onion, minced
2 cups celery, diagonally sliced
1/2 clove garlic, minced
1/2 tsp. dried tarragon leaves
1/2 tsp. dried basil leaves
1 tsp. dried parsley flakes
Freshly ground pepper to taste
1 cup long grain rice, uncooked
1/2 Tbs. granulated chicken bouillon
2 cups boiling water
3 cans (6 1/2 oz. ea.) chopped clams
1 1/2 cups frozen peas, thawed

Heat the wine or stock and sauté the onion, celery, garlic and seasonings until crisp-tender. Add the rice and boiling water and bring back to a boil. Stir gently with a fork and simmer on low, covered, for 15 minutes. Add clams and peas and simmer, covered, about 10 minutes more or until the rice has absorbed all liquid and is tender.

Yield: About 8 cups
Total Fat Grams: 4

CRABMEAT AND MUSHROOMS

When serving this dish you may want to sprinkle fresh, minced parsley on top and surround the crabmeat with wedges of lemon. This is a very attractive hot appetizer for guests.

Pam or other spray-on oil
1 pound mushrooms, coarsely chopped
1 cup green onions, chopped
18 cherry tomatoes, halved
1 pound fresh or frozen crabmeat, thawed and flaked
2 Tbs. fresh lemon juice
6 Tbs. dry sherry
1/8 tsp. sugar

Treat the pan with spray-on oil for 2-1/2 seconds. Sauté the mushrooms and green onions on high, stirring briskly for 1 minute. Add a dash of white wine or sherry if more moisture is needed. Add all remaining ingredients. Cook on medium, stirring until heated through. Serve on steamed rice.

Yield: About 6 cups
Total Fat Grams: 9

CRAB AND CHEESE BAKE

4 Tbs. dry white wine or defatted chicken stock
1 cup celery, sliced
1/2 cup onion, sliced
1/2 cup carrot, sliced thin
1/2 cup mushrooms, sliced thin
1/2 cup diced bell pepper, diced
1 can (32 oz.) whole tomatoes, broken up, with juice
1 1/2 cups fresh or frozen crab meat, flaked
1 cup cooked rice
1/4 tsp. salt
1 tsp. sugar
1 bay leaf
1/2 cup fat-free cheddar cheese

Sauté the celery, onion, carrot, mushrooms and green pepper until tender. Add the remaining ingredients, except the cheese. Simmer 5 minutes and remove the bay leaf. Move to oven-proof baking dish and bake at 350° for 15 minutes. Sprinkle cheese on top and reheat until the cheese melts.

Yield: 8 cups
Total Fat Grams: 5

SCALLOPS CACCIATORE

3 Tbs. white wine
1 medium onion, chopped
1 medium green bell pepper, chopped
1 clove garlic, minced
1 can (16 oz.) tomatoes, drained
1 can (8 oz.) tomato sauce
1 pound bay scallops
1/4 cup dry white wine
2 bay leaves
Salt and freshly ground pepper
A pinch of hot red pepper flakes
2 Tbs. fresh parsley, chopped

Sauté the onion, green pepper and garlic in 3 Tbs. wine until tender. Add all other ingredients, breaking up the tomatoes with a spoon. Simmer until the scallops are cooked through. Serve on pasta.

Yield: About 6 cups
Total Fat Grams: 5

STIR-FRIED CRAB AND MUSHROOMS

4 Tbs. dry white wine or vegetable stock
1/2 pound mushrooms, cut in quarters
1/2 cup green onions, chopped
12 cherry tomatoes, halved
1/2 pound fresh or frozen crabmeat, flaked
3 Tbs. sweet vermouth or medium-sweet sherry
1 Tbs. fresh lemon juice
Steamed rice

Place your wok over high heat and stir-fry the mushrooms and green onions for one minute. Add the tomatoes, crabmeat, vermouth and lemon juice. Stir-fry until heated through. Serve over rice.

Yield: About 3 cups
Total Fat Grams: 3

SCALLOPS IN TERIYAKI SAUCE

1 tsp. sugar
2 tsp. sake or dry white wine
1 Tbs. cream sherry
2 Tbs. soy sauce
1/4 cup all-purpose flour
1/2 tsp. white pepper
1 pound sea scallops
Spray-on oil

Stir together the sugar, sake, sherry and soy sauce until the sugar is dissolved. Set aside. In a small plastic bag combine the flour and pepper. Toss each scallop in the bag to coat with the flour leaving a thin coating of flour mixture. Place a non-stick pan over high heat and spray with 5 seconds of spray-on oil. Sauté the scallops in the pan about 1 to 1 1/2 minutes per side. Remove from the pan. Add the sugar mixture to the pan and cook, stirring constantly until the mixture thickens slightly. Replace scallops and toss well. Serve on rice.

Yield: About 2 cups
Total Fat Grams: 6

STEAMED OR POACHED FISH

Preparing fish is quick and easy. Especially if there is a microwave handy. Fish can steam in the microwave without any added water. Simply place in a microwaveable plate with the thickest part of the fish on the outside, the thinner part toward the middle. Cover tightly with plastic wrap leaving a pleat in the middle for expansion. Be sure to turn fish steaks or fillets at least once during cooking. Test for doneness with a fork to see if the flesh flakes easily and is opaque rather than translucent. The fish will continue to cook at the center for about 5 minutes after removal from the oven.

Cook with some lemon, wine, vinegar, ginger, onions and/or garlic to minimize odor and fishy taste. The time varies with the density and thickness of the fillet or steak and the particular microwave, so start off with a minimum amount of time and increase as necessary. You'll grow accustomed to your own oven and become a master fish chef.

There are other methods of preparing fish that enhance the flavors and the textures, such as stews, bakes, curries and the Oriental or Italian and Greek influences.

The fat grams in fish vary from sole, 1 gram per 4 ounces, raw, to mackerel at 15 grams for 4 ounces, raw. There are different kinds of salmon, mackerel and tuna, so check the variety and your counter book for accuracy.

In recipes of your own, substitute Buttery Spray and Olive Oil Spray to keep the fat gram count low. The fish is already low in fat, enhance this delicacy with condiments that will keep it low in fat.

BAKED HERBED FISH

2 pounds red snapper or halibut
Weight Watchers Buttery Spray
1/2 tsp. salt
1/2 tsp. marjoram
1/2 tsp. thyme leaves
1/4 tsp. garlic powder
1/8 tsp. white pepper
2 bay leaves
1/2 cup onion, chopped
Paprika
1/2 cup white wine
Lime or lemon wedges

Wash fish, pat dry and put in a baking dish. Spray with Buttery Spray, about 5 seconds, both sides. Combine all seasonings except the bay leaves, onion and paprika. Sprinkle the combined seasonings over the fish. Top with the bay leaves and onion, sprinkle with paprika. Pour wine over all. Bake uncovered at 350° for 20 to 30 minutes or until the fish flakes easily with a fork. Serve with the lime or lemon wedges.

Yield: 4 servings, 8 ounces each serving
Total Fat Grams: 14, if red snapper; 22, if halibut

FISH ISLAND BAKE

1/4 cup white wine or defatted stock
1 small onion, chopped
1/2 cup celery, chopped
1/2 medium green pepper, chopped
1 1/2 pounds snapper or grouper
Juice of large fresh lime
12 saltines, crushed
Salt and pepper to taste

Sauté the onion, celery and green pepper in the wine or stock until tender. Cut the fish in cubes and add remaining ingredients to the sautéed vegetables in a medium casserole dish. Mix well, cover and bake at 350° for 50 minutes. Remove the cover and bake 10 minutes more.

Yield: About 6 cups
Total Fat Grams: 12

SWORDFISH AND BALSAMIC VINEGAR

4 swordfish steaks, 6 oz. ea.
Salt and freshly ground pepper
1/2 cup flour
Olive Oil Pam
1 cup bottled clam juice
3 Tbs. balsamic vinegar
2 Tbs. dry white wine
1 Tbs. fresh rosemary, chopped
1 1/2 tsp. fresh thyme, chopped
1 clove garlic, minced
Juice of 1/2 lemon + 4 wedges
1/4 cup fresh parsley, chopped

Season the fish steaks, both sides, with salt and pepper. Dredge the fish in flour and shake off the excess. Heat an oven-proof pan, apply Pam (2-1/2 second spray) and brown the swordfish steaks over medium heat. If necessary spray again to avoid sticking. Remove the steaks and set aside. Add 1/2 cup clam juice, vinegar, wine and rosemary, thyme and garlic to the pan and boil the mixture for 1 minute. Return the fish to the pan and bake at 350° for 10 minutes. Pour the remaining clam juice and the lemon juice over the fish and bake for 8 to 10 minutes more. Transfer the fish to plates. Boil the juices left in the pan to reduce until 1/2 cup is left. Strain and pour over the fish. Garnish with lemon wedges and parsley.

Yield: 4 swordfish steaks
Total Fat Grams: 34

SOLE OR FLOUNDER WITH CAPERS

1 pound sole or flounder
Weight Watchers Buttery Spray
3 Tbs. capers
Freshly ground black pepper

Place the flounder or sole in a baking dish, spray with 2-1/2 seconds of Buttery Spray, add capers and freshly ground pepper to taste. Cover with plastic wrap and cook in the microwave according to directions in Steamed Or Poached Fish (page 332).

Yield: 2 servings, 8 ounces each
Total Fat Grams: 6

FISH STEW

1/2 cup dry lentils
1/2 cup dried split peas
1 can (15 oz.) stewed tomatoes
1 small onion, minced
1/2 medium green bell pepper, minced
1 carrot, finely chopped
1 rib celery, minced
1 pound salmon or tuna, cubed
1 can (16 oz.) northern white or navy beans with liquid
1 package (10 oz.) frozen corn kernels
Freshly ground pepper

In a large pot bring 2 cups water to boil with the lentils, split peas, tomatoes, onion, pepper, carrot and celery. Simmer, covered, for 25 minutes. Add the fish, beans and corn. Add water to cover, if necessary. Cover and simmer for 15 minutes or until the lentils and peas are cooked through. Season to taste with pepper.

Yield: About 10 cups
Total Fat Grams: 43, if red sockeye salmon; 21, if chum salmon; 20, if yellowfin tuna; 99, if bluefin tuna

FRESH TUNA ON PASTA

2 cans (16 oz. ea.) whole tomatoes, drained and chopped
2 Tbs. tomato paste
1 medium onion, chopped
1 pound fresh yellowfin tuna, 1/4 inch thick
Freshly ground black pepper
1/2 cup fresh mixed herbs, minced
2 cloves garlic, minced
2 Tbs. capers, minced
1 pound twisted, eggless macaroni

In a large no-stick pan cook tomatoes and onion over medium heat, stirring often for 20 minutes. Cool slightly and puree in a blender. Season the tuna with black pepper and sauté in the hot non-stick pan over medium heat for 3 to 4 minutes. Add a spoon of the tomato mixture if the tuna begins to stick. Add the mixed herbs, garlic, capers and tomato puree. Cook 2 minutes. Cook the pasta. Drain the liquid, reserving 1 cup. Place pasta in a large serving bowl and cover in sauce. If the sauce is too thick, add some reserved liquid from the pasta to reach the desired consistency.

Yield: About 12 cups
Total Fat Grams: 20

QUICKIE TUNA PASTA

1 cup + 1 Tbs. broth or defatted stock
1 clove garlic, crushed
2 cans (6 oz. ea.) water-packed tuna, drained
1/4 cup fresh lemon juice
3 Tbs. capers
1 can (6 oz.) tomato paste
1 Tbs. cornstarch
2 Tbs. water

Sauté the garlic in 1 Tbs. broth. Add the tuna and remaining ingredients except the cornstarch and water. Cook together 20 to 30 minutes. If necessary, for thickening, gradually add the cornstarch, which has been dissolved in the water, to thicken. Serve on eggless pasta of your choice. Season with salt and pepper.

Yield: About 4 cups
Total Fat Grams: 7

COD WITH TOMATOES AND FENNEL

1/2 tsp. fennel seeds
2 Tbs. defatted chicken stock
1 large fresh fennel bulb, cut in half, cored and chopped fine
1 large leek, white and tender green parts, chopped fine
2 garlic cloves, minced
1 can (28 oz.) plum tomatoes, chopped coarse, with liquid
1/2 tsp. finely grated orange zest
1 bay leaf
Salt and fresh ground pepper
4 6-oz. cod fillets, 1/4" thick
2 Tbs. fresh basil, chopped fine

With a mortar and pestle or grinder, grind the fennel seeds or finely chop with a knife. Set aside. Heat the defatted stock in a non-stick skillet and add the fresh fennel, leek and garlic. Cover the skillet and cook over moderate heat, stirring occasionally, until the veggies are translucent, about 5 minutes. Add the tomato with the liquid, the ground fennel seed, orange zest, bay leaf and a pinch of salt and pepper. Bring to a boil. Lower the heat and simmer for 20 minutes, stirring occasionally, until the sauce thickens slightly. Place the cod fillets in the pan, covering with a bit of the sauce, and simmer until the fish is cooked through, about 8 to 10 minutes. Remove the fish and cover to keep warm. Discard the bay leaf and proceed to boil the sauce to thicken, about 3 minutes. Stir in the basil, season to taste and spoon the sauce over the fish.

Yield: 4 fillets
Total Fat Grams: 12

Miscellaneous Goodies

One of the hazards of a weight-loss diet is the feeling of denial which results from the abstinence from desserts or sweet-tasting goodies. While we all start with the willpower to control our appetites, the need for the foods that "feel good" is overpowering. As mentioned earlier in this book, in the paragraph describing the yo-yo syndrome, these desires for forbidden foods can lead to frustration, followed by abandonment of control, leading to a binge, followed by guilt. The cycle is damaging and we become victim to our own lack of self-forgiveness. It sounds painful...and it is!

This section of recipes is a happy solution to the cravings for self-indulgence to which we are prey...and yet we can remain true to the low-fat lifestyle. Most of these recipes are entirely free of fat and will give you that satisfaction of indulging yourself without guilt.

It's a good idea to browse through your supermarket in search of some of the fat-free cookies and desserts or low-fat and fat-free ice cream substitutes that are appearing in prolific numbers as the low-fat approach to eating becomes more popular. However, remember to enjoy these treats in moderation. If two or three fat-free cookies will not do the trick, you are not eating them to satisfy a craving for sweets but you are hungry enough for some real food and should switch to a heartier snack or light meal.

STRAWBERRY SORBET

1 cup sugar
1 cup hot water
2 Tbs. fresh lemon juice
1 Tbs. orange juice
1 pint hulled strawberries

Dissolve the sugar in hot water and cool completely. Add the juices and place in a blender with the strawberries. Blend until smooth. Place in the freezer in an appropriate container and freeze until almost firm. Blend again and freeze until hard.

Yield: About 2 to 3 cups
Total Fat Grams: 0

PEAR SORBET WITH RASPBERRY SAUCE

4 cans (16 oz. ea.) sliced pears, unsweetened
1 Tbs. honey
1 package (10 oz.) frozen raspberries

Arrange the pears in 1 gallon plastic self-sealing bags in a single layer. Freeze until frozen solid (overnight). Place the frozen pears in a food processor with the honey and blend until smooth, but still icy. Do not allow the mixture to melt. Store in the freezer until serving time, however, plan on running through the food processor again if the mixture is too frozen. The consistency should be icy smooth, similar to sherbet. Thaw the raspberries in the microwave on defrost. Puree in the food processor or blender and strain to remove the seeds. Serve over the sorbet.

Yield: About 6 cups
Total Fat Grams: 0

DRESSED UP ANGEL

1 package angel food cake mix
1/3 cup cocoa
2 tsp. instant coffee (dry) or instant espresso

Prepare angel food mix according to package directions, adding the cocoa and coffee to the dry mix. Beat for 1 1/2 minutes, scraping the bowl often. Bake at 350° in an unoiled tube pan for 40 to 50 minutes. Serve with vanilla or coffee fat-free ice cream.

Yield: 1 cake
Total Fat Grams: 5

APPLE BAKE

2 cups Granny Smith apples, sliced
2 Tbs. cinnamon
4 Tbs. sugar
1 Tbs. ground nutmeg
Weight Watchers Buttery Spray
2 Tbs. fresh lemon juice

Combine the apple slices and dry ingredients. Spray for about 2 1/2 seconds with the Buttery Spray and add the lemon juice. Toss and place in a glass bowl in the microwave, covered with vented plastic wrap. Cook on high for about 2 to 3 minutes or until the apples are warm and crisp-tender. Serve with fat-free ice cream or whipped topping.

Yield: About 2 cups
Total Fat Grams: 2

PRUNE WHIP

1 pound prunes
Water to cover
3 lemon slices

Cover the prunes and lemon slices in the water, bring to a boil and lower the heat immediately. Cook on low until the prunes puff up. Allow the prunes to cool, then remove the pits and the lemon slices. Whip the prunes and whatever water is left in a blender until smooth and creamy. Chill.

Yield: About 6 cups
Total Fat Grams: 0

CRANBERRY FRUIT RELISH

1 package fresh cranberries, washed
4 to 5 unpeeled apples, cored
1/4 cup honey to taste
2 small oranges, peeled

Place cranberries with oranges in a food processor and blend until finely chopped. Grate the apples in a blender and mix with the cranberry-orange mixture. Add honey to taste.

Yield: About 5 cups
Total Fat Grams: 0

MARVELOUS CARROT MUFFINS

2 cups whole wheat flour
1 cup sugar
1 tsp. baking powder
1 tsp. baking soda
2 tsp. ground cinnamon
1/2 tsp. salt
1 can (8 oz.) crushed pineapple, undrained
6 egg whites, at room temperature
2 cups shredded carrots
2/3 cup raisins

In a large bowl, mix all dry ingredients with a fork. Beat the egg whites until frothy. Add the egg whites, carrots, pineapple and juice to the dry ingredients. Mix until thoroughly blended. Add raisins and mix again. Spoon into muffin tins that have been treated with spray-on oil or into cupcake papers placed in the tin. Bake at 350° for 45 minutes, or until a toothpick inserted in the center comes out clean.

Yield: About 12 small muffins or 6 jumbo muffins
Total Fat Grams: 6

BRAN MUFFINS

1 cup all-purpose flour
2 cups Nabisco 100% bran
1/4 cup corn meal
1 tsp. salt
1/3 cup non-fat powdered milk
1 cup water
1 tsp. baking soda
1/4 cup Egg Beaters
1/2 cup molasses
2 Tbs. dates, chopped
2/3 cup raisins

Combine all ingredients. Spoon into muffin tins that have been treated with spray-on oil or lined with cupcake papers. Bake for 20 to 25 minutes at 325°, or until a toothpick inserted in the center comes out clean.

Yield: About 12 muffins
Total Fat Grams: 5

RAISIN BRAN MUFFINS

4 cups raisin bran or bran flakes
2 1/2 cups all-purpose flour
1 1/2 cups sugar
2 1/2 tsp. baking soda
1 tsp. salt
1/2 cup Egg Beaters
2 cups applesauce
1/2 cup liquid Butter Buds
1 cup raisins (optional)

In a large bowl, mix all dry ingredients. Add the liquid ingredients and mix well. It takes a good bit of mixing to get all the dry ingredients thoroughly blended and covered with the wet. You may have to use your bare hands! If you've used bran flakes, you will want to add the raisins. I like both the raisin bran and the extras. Bake at 400° for 15 to 20 minutes in muffin tins that have been sprayed with Pam or with which you've used paper muffin liners.

Yield: 2 dozen regular-sized muffins or 9 large
Total Fat Grams: 3

BLUEBERRY BRAN MUFFINS

1 cup wheat bran
1 cup whole wheat flour
1/4 cup unprocessed oat bran
1 1/4 tsp. ground cinnamon
1 tsp. baking soda
1/4 cup very ripe banana, mashed
1/4 cup herb-flavored honey
2 egg whites, unbeaten
1 tsp. vanilla extract
1 cup low-fat buttermilk
1 cup fresh or frozen blueberries, coarsely chopped

In a medium bowl mix together all dry ingredients. Set aside. In a large bowl, whisk the banana, honey, egg whites and vanilla. Whisk in the buttermilk. Stir the liquid mixture into the dry ingredients until barely combined. Fold in the berries. Spoon into muffin cups treated with spray-on oil or lined with cupcake papers. Bake for 20 to 30 minutes at 375° or until muffins spring bake when gently pressed.

Yield: About 12 muffins
Total Fat Grams: 10

KARO FAT-FREE CHOCOLATE CAKE

Spray-on oil
1 1/4 cups flour
1 cup sugar
1/2 cup unsweetened cocoa
1/4 cup cornstarch
1/2 tsp. baking soda
1/2 tsp. salt
4 egg whites, unbeaten
1 cup water
1/2 cup Karo Corn Syrup

Treat a 9-inch square baking pan with spray-on oil. In a large bowl, combine the dry ingredients. Mix well. In a medium bowl, whisk the egg whites, water and corn syrup. Stir into the dry ingredients until smooth. Pour into the prepared pan and bake at 350° for 30 minutes or until the cake springs back when gently pressed. Cool on wire rack for 10 minutes.

Yield: 1 cake
Total Fat Grams: 0

SPICE COOKIES

This is a two-day recipe so be prepared to start the day before you intend to bake them!

2 3/4 cups flour
1 tsp. cinnamon
1 tsp. ground cloves
1 tsp. allspice
1/2 tsp. baking soda
1/2 cup herbed honey
1/2 cup molasses
3/4 cup brown sugar
2 egg whites, unbeaten
1 Tbs. fresh lemon juice
1 tsp. grated lemon rind
1/2 tsp. grated orange rind
3 Tbs. raisins

Stir flour with spices and baking soda. Set aside. Bring the honey, molasses and brown sugar to a boil. Place in a large bowl and cool to lukewarm. Stir in egg whites and juice, then grated rind. Stir in flour mixture gradually and then work in the raisins. Cover and chill overnight. Roll dough in small batches on a floured board, 1/4 inch thick. Keep remainder of dough chilled as you work. Cut dough into rectangles and place 1 inch apart on a cookie sheet treated with spray-on oil. Bake at 400° for 10 to 12 minutes.

Yield: About 24 rectangles
Total Fat Grams: 3

ORANGE SMOOTHIE

1 can (6 oz.) frozen orange juice concentrate
1 cup skim milk
1/2 cup water
1/2 cup sugar
1 Tbs. vanilla extract

Combine all ingredients in a blender, add 1 tray crushed ice and blend again. For variety add strawberries or banana.

Yield: About 3 cups
Total Fat Grams: 0; 1, if banana added

PEACH STRAWBERRY COOLER

1 cup fresh or frozen strawberries
2 cups pineapple juice
1 cup diced peaches, skinned
1 Tbs. honey

Whiz all ingredients in the blender until smooth.

Yield: About 4 cups
Total Fat Grams: 0

PINEAPPLE-PEACH YOGI

1 cup pineapple juice
1 cup orange juice
1 cup nonfat yogurt
2 cups frozen peaches

Whiz all ingredients in the blender until smooth.

Yield: About 5 cups
Total Fat Grams: 0

STRAWBERRY BANANA SHAKE

2 cups pineapple juice
2 cups fresh strawberries
1 ripe banana
Honey to taste

Blend all ingredients together until smooth. Serve with a strawberry on top for added panache.

Yield: About 5 cups
Total Fat Grams: 1

THE BERRY GOOD PARFAIT

3 1/2 cups fresh strawberries, divided
1 cup champagne
1/3 cup sugar
1 cup fresh blackberries
1 cup fresh blueberries
1 cup fresh raspberries
1 quart fat-free vanilla ice cream, softened

Place 2 cups strawberries in a blender or food processor and whip until smooth. Transfer to a saucepan with the champagne and the sugar, and stir. Bring to a boil, reduce heat and cook, uncovered for 30 minutes or until the mixture is reduced to 1 cup. Stir occasionally. Slice the remaining strawberries in half and combine with the other berries in a medium bowl. Add the champagne mixture and toss gently. Swirl 1/2 cup of the berry mixture through the ice cream and place about 1/2 cup in each of 8 parfait glasses. Top with the berry mixture, cover and freeze for about 30 minutes and serve.

Yield: 8 Parfaits
Total Fat Grams: 5

HOT FUDGE SUNDAE

2 Tbs. fat-free chocolate fudge ice cream topping
1 slice Karo Fat Free Chocolate Cake (page 353)
1 to 2 scoops fat free vanilla ice cream
1 maraschino cherry (optional)

Place the fudge topping in a small container in the microwave until heated. Place the cake on a small dessert plate. Top with the ice cream and pour the fudge sauce over all. You may want to top this masterpiece with the maraschino cherry reminiscent of the old ice cream parlor sundae of years gone by.

Yield: 1 sundae
Total Fat Grams: About 1

CHAPTER X

THE END...OF THE BEGINNING

Now, there you have it, my friend! It's simple. It's adaptable. And it's effective.

Acquiring a new aproach to your life, to the foods you crave and to the treats that turn you on, is now only a matter of a smattering of self-determination and a foray into the supermarkets and health stores in your area. The shelves are stocked with low-fat foods and fat-free edibles that are a wonderful result of modern technology, from fat-free cream cheese and mayonnaise to fat-free ice cream and cake. Combine these extras with a basic menu of fruits, veggies, pastas and beans, and you'll never again long for the wrong stuff.

And to help keep you motivated, there are some publications that you may be interested in reading to expose you to ideas from others who are enjoying this low-fat lifestyle. Gabe Mirkin, an M.D. in Silver Spring, Maryland has a show on WRC radio, on which he advocates this way of eating. His book, *Getting Thin*, published by Little Brown, explains the physiology of gaining and losing weight and of fat in the body. He has a monthly newsletter available, *The Mirkin Report*, which you can subscribe to, as well, at Box 6608, Silver Spring, Maryland 20916.

You will find a vast array of fascinating health-oriented articles in *Prevention*, available from Rodale Press in Emmaus, Pennsylvania and *American Health*, published by RD Publications in New York.

The finest and most informative of the newsletters I've come across is *Nutrition Action Healthletter* published by Center for Science in the Public Interest, Suite 300, 1875 Connecticut Avenue, N.W., Washington, D.C. 20009-5728. The information is entertainingly presented and a neat way to continue learning more of what you'll want to know as you become more involved in this exciting new lifestyle.

These and a number of other magazines and newsletters are devoting more and more space to the concept of the low-fat regimen and its benefits in keeping one younger...looking and feeling.

Your goal of achieving the new, slimmer, healthier you, who is more fit and raring to go, is just a few weeks away from the first day of your low-fat lifestyle. Before you know it your friends will be following your lead. And when you have the opportunity to return to the days of gorging on the breakfast totaling 125 grams of fat, and lunch of 85 grams, with a dinner topping out at about 97 grams (with dessert, of course), you'll wonder why you would—or—how you could. You're not missing any of the good life with your new style of life. What a wonderful way to get healthy!

Instead, with a smug look of satisfaction, you pat your lean tummy and grin. You've been beaten up by articles and books extolling lowering fat in your diet and your doctor has admonished you for your girth or cholesterol readings at every visit. You have learned how to convince your body that you're eating as you always have, but without the "bad stuff" and you've enjoyed the process! While "they" told you that you had to learn to "eat to live" instead of enjoying a life of "living to eat" you've learned how to have the time of your life...LIVING & LOVING LOW FAT!

DO YOU HAVE THE URGE TO...

CONTRIBUTE to the well-being of others? See your name in print? Be an important and credited part of my next book and the LIVING & LOVING LOWFAT NEWSLETTER by sending your own recipes that are easy-to-prepare and low-fat. All ideas and new-fangled, low-fat tricks are welcome. Please write:

Tree Stevens
P. O. Box 1017
Greenbelt, MD 20768-1017

LIVING & LOVING LOWFAT NEWSLETTER

Now that you have an approach to your new low-fat lifestyle you surely want to remain aware of all the new goodies that are available and the information that can help you to tow the low-fat line. We know how important this updated information is to you. To keep the low-fat lifestyle exciting and fun, for continuing information regarding fat-free and low-fat products, and to present to you new recipes, many from our own readers, that taste great and fill that need for good-eating, we offer to you our newsletter.

Send $24.00 for one year's subscription to:

LIVING & LOVING LOWFAT
P. O. Box 1017
Greenbelt, MD 20768-1017

INDEX

T

V

W

Z

I met Tree about six years ago and she continues to inspire me. Her eating lifestyle is just plain common sense. Her recipes are low in fat, tasty and can be made from ingredients normally found in your kitchen. I have dozens of cookbooks, but Tree's is always the first one I reach for.

The beauty of Tree's book is that it is not a diet, it is an easy to follow eating lifestyle. I believe we all want to maintain a healthy eating style, but in most cases we are not willing to give up taste or abundance to achieve it. The great news is with Tree's recipes, you don't have to! I just wish I had met Tree twenty years ago!

Kathy Giordano

Fairfax, Virginia

When I first saw Tree's book, it was like I had struck gold. One of the challenges to living a vegetarian lifestyle is variety and wonderful flavors. Tree's book has both. In addition, the recipes are easy and quick which fits very nicely into the lifestyle of most of today's modern families.

After reading and trying so many of the recipes, I wanted to share them with all of my friends. You no doubt will feel the same way as you wander through these pages abundant with healthy new dishes.

Brenda Chowdhury

San Antonio, Texas